AF696849

HOW TO WIN, DELAY, REDUCE OR ELIMINATE LAWSUITS FOR MONEY WITHOUT A LAWYER

FINANCIAL MANAGEMENT ASSOCIATES, INC.
3824 East Indian School Rd. Phoenix, Arizona 85018

This publication is designed to provide accurate and authoritative information in regard to the subject matter covered. It is sold with the understanding that the publisher is not engaged in rendering legal, accounting or other professional service. If legal advice or other expert assistance is required, the services of a competent professional person should be sought.

--From a Declaration of Principles jointly adopted by a Committee of the American Bar Association and a Committee of Publishers.

Library of Congress Cataloging in Publication
Data Main Entry Under Title:

HOW TO WIN, DELAY, REDUCE OR ELIMINATE
LAWSUITS FOR MONEY WITHOUT A LAWYER

FINANCIAL MANAGEMENT ASSOCIATES, INC.
3824 East Indian School Rd., Phoenix, Arizona 85018

ISBN 0-930566-06-8

TABLE OF CONTENTS

PREFACE

The judicial system in this country has been under intensive "study" and "reform" since 1904! The lawyers, judges, politicians and law professors just talk--talk--talk; they organize committees and write impressive "Reports." But the damn system has simply broken down and there appears to be little chance of improvement even though the Chief Justice of the United States has been yelling and screaming at lawyers for years to get their act together.

Many lawyers charge $100 to $400 or more per hour for their "legal services." And all lawyers have "short hours" and "long hours" in setting their fees -- if you get my meaning! Cases drag on and on and on, ad infinitum -- and legal fees just keep rolling in, on and on. And the bad part is that the modern trial is more a "gladiator's" duel in which the lawyers have one eye on the grand stands -- the other eye on their own pocketbook, and somehow the interests of the client -- the American litigant -- gets altogether lost in the "fascination with procedures." Gone With The Wind!

A recent magazine article described the current situation as follows:

> In the past few years, the costs of litigation have skyrocketed as companies are hit with more lawsuits that take longer to complete. Delays, always notorious in the legal process, have grown worse. And judges themselves have been pressed into playing a new role in American society, often supplanting elected officials in trying to settle the country's most intractable problems. Indeed, as the U. S. moves from a free enterprise state to a regulatory state, litigation becomes a primary method of treating all socially significant problems.
>
> But all solutions will necessarily be piecemeal because they respond to a multifaceted problem with no single or simple root cause. Any general strategy to combat the rising tide of litigation must take account of technological and demographic changes, a vast wave of new legislation, and a judicial revolution that has produced thousands of new claims and new plaintiffs.
>
> "The Chilling Impact of Litigation: Easier access to the courts means skyrocketing costs and interminable delays," Legal Affairs, Business Week, June 6, 1977, pages 58, 59.

The end result is that one of society's most "noble" professions (not a unanimous designation) has utterly failed in its formost obligations to society; lawyers have not only failed to take any definitive measures to improve -- or "reform" -- the system -- they stand around -- in a lackadaisical stupor -- and watch the courts become a "pork barrel" for less than "ethical" persons and a bonanza for the "rich cats" who have an inside track on the big fees, most of which is ultimately paid by consumers and taxpayers -- you and me!

Now, what to do? Well, let's join them. Yes, You Can Be Your Own Lawyer In Court. If it takes a typical case one--two--three or more years to wind its way through the court system and costs both litigants a fortune -- why can't you simply learn these cute little "procedures" the lawyers are so "fascinated" with and bring your case to a close in maybe four--five--or more years -- or never? If you learn all the "techniques" the lawyers use routinely to "drag out" cases, you can (1) have a hellava lot of fun, (2) save a bundle in legal fees and expenses, (3) save money on the case by settling on your own terms, (4) save it all by winning the case, and (5) generally have a blast by kicking up a lot of hell just for the hell of it!

But, let's get one thing straight: When you get sued in court, let's have no more of the "nice guy" crap. When a dispute gets to court it's time to roll up your sleeves, put on the iron knuckles and "cut the bastards up in little bitty pieces and scatter them all over the courthouse floor." Don't get sucked into believing the Turkey who sued you is gonna' turn out to be a friend of yours. No. I guarantee you: He will kick you in the butt at every turn -- and his jack-legged lawyer will cut your throat at the drop of a hat. Second, play the "game" strictly in accordance with the rules and the law. That's what this book is all about. Keep your cool! Third, be ethical, honest, but tough.

When you get sued here's what you do: Study this book carefully -- do your research -- get fully prepared -- and slowly start turning the screws on that Turkey Plaintiff, and make him -- and his jack-legged lawyer -- wish they'd never heard of you. With the proper use of discovery "techniques" and trial "tactics" you can be in command all the way. Carefully schedule your pleadings, discovery, hearings, and procedures to conform with your interests and desires -- and convenience -- and watch them squirm and squiggle -- and wear the bastards down to a frazzle.

You can really have a ball, enjoy yourself and save a bunch.

What about pro se (in person; in his own behalf; do it yourself) litigation rather than paying a "professional" to handle your case? Voltaire once said:

> Only twice in my life have I felt utterly ruined: once when I lost a lawsuit and once when I won.

A recent law review article suggests:

> Too often, the bar and the bench have regarded, treated, and disposed of those who proceed without counsel as, at best, outsiders. As a result all parties lose -- not only the pro se petitioner, but also those who presume that the pro se petitioner has a worthless claim, or worse, that he

> himself is somehow worthless because he has no counsel. There are those who recognize that the opportunity to proceed without counsel in our system prevents a strangle-hold on justice by lawyers. (Emphasis added)
>
> Pro Se Litigation: The Misunderstood Pro Se Litigant: More Than A Pawn In The Game by John P. Flannery and Ira P. Robbins, 41 Brooklyn Law Review 769, Spring 1975.

The libraries are filled with books that pronounce the greatness of our American way of life -- including our judicial system -- and there are an equal number of books that blast the court system as "rotten to the roots."

This book doesn't take off on any of those trails; we tell you how to come out a winner when you go to court. That's what this book is about.

CHAPTER I

YOUR RIGHT TO DEFEND YOURSELF IN COURT

You have a legal right to represent yourself -- be your own lawyer -- in court. Our society has recently experienced some unusual traumas with lawyers--judges--courts--politicians and unethical scoundrels. Although lawyers may not be the "sole" cause of these phenomena, they surely led the parade! Our laws (thousands of them) and our courts (thousands of them) don't seem to be able to keep the barn door shut; and when it swings open -- all hell breaks loose! All the Kings Men can't put them back in the barn.

Mistrust of lawyers, courts and judges was one of the major considerations that motivated the Founding Fathers to write the Federal Constitution as they did. The U. S. Supreme Court recently said:

> In the American Colonies the insistence upon a right of self-representation was, if anything, more fervent than in England.
>
> The colonists brought with them an appreciation of the virtues of self-reliance and a traditional distrust of lawyers. When the Colonies were first settled, "the lawyer was synonymous with the cringing Attorneys-General and Solicitors-General of the Crown and the arbitrary Justices of the King's

> Court, all bent on the conviction of those who opposed the King's prerogatives, and twisting the law to secure convictions." This prejudice gained strength in the Colonies where "distrust of lawyers became an institution." Several Colonies prohibited pleading for hire in the 17th century. The prejudice persisted into the 18th century as "the lower classes came to identify lawyers with the upper class." The years of Revolution and Confederation saw an upsurge of antilawyer sentiment, a "sudden revival, after the War of the Revolution, of the old dislike and distrust of lawyers as a class." In the heat of these sentiments the Constitution was forged.
>
> This is not to say that the Colonies were slow to recognize the value of counsel in criminal cases. Colonial judges soon departed from ancient English practice and allowed accused felons the aid of counsel for their defense. At the same time, however, the basic right of self-representation was never questioned. We have found no instance where a colonial court required a defendant in a criminal case to accept as his representative an unwanted lawyer. Indeed, even where counsel was permitted, the general practice continued to be self-representation.
>
> Faretta v. California, 422 U.S. 806 (1975)

On May 27, 1977, Chief Justice Berger, at an American Bar Association Conference told the lawyers what he thought about the "legal profession." A newspaper article, May 28, 1977, told the story as follows:

> "Chief Justice Warren E. Berger warned Friday that unless more legal disputes are settled outside the courtroom the United States could be "overrun by hordes of lawyers hungry as locusts."
>
> Berger, an advocate of court reform, turned his attention to the legal profession in a speech to the American Bar Association, contending that lawyers, judges

> and law professors had developed a "fascination with procedure" that may have led.....to a smug assumption that conflicts can be solved only by law-trained people."
>
> Non-lawyers, he suggested, could help settle many disputes cheaper and faster.
>
> "The harsh truth is that unless we devise substitutes for the courtroom processes, we may be on our way to a society overrun by hordes of lawyers hungry as locusts and brigades of judges in numbers never before contemplated," he said.
>
> The Chief Justice's remarks were made in a speech at an ABA conference in New York on new ways to settle "minor" legal disputes -- such as small claims, landlord-tenant conflicts and consumer complaints. A copy of the text was made available in Washington."

An assembly sponsored by the American Bar Association recently reported about the American probate system that:

> "The bar should encourage the trend toward various devices permitting settlement of estates with little or no court involvement (in the absence of controversy) and with only minimally necessary involvement of lawyers. The development of procedures for transferring property without administration should be encouraged, as should "do-it-yourself techniques."
>
> American Bar Association Journal, January, 1977, page 88.

During the past few years our court system has continued to deteriorate -- rather than improve -- and it is more overcrowded now than ever before -- the cases are clogging the court calendars -- and the legal system simply can't seem to cope with the proliferation of litigation.

See, for example, "The Chilling Impact of Litigation, Easier Access to the Courts Means Skyrocketing Costs and Interminable Delays," Legal Affairs, Business Week, June 6, 1977, page 58.

In response to this unmanageable situation there has recently been made available to the general public a wide variety of do-it-yourself legal guides covering such subjects as How To Avoid Probate, How To Form Your Own Corporation, How To Win Landlord-Tenant Disputes, How To Write Your Own Will, and many others.

This book has been planned, designed, written and published to help you handle your own case in court without a lawyer and without staggering legal fees and expenses, and to avoid getting overrun "by the hordes."

With respect to your legal right to represent yourself in court without a lawyer, the United States Supreme Court, in the Faretta Case, supra, said:

> In the federal courts, the right of self-representation has been protected by statute since the beginnings of our Nation. Section 35 of the Judiciary Act of 1789, 1 Stat. 73, 92, enacted by the First Congress and signed by President Washington one day before the Sixth Amendment was proposed, provided that 'in all the courts of the United States, the parties may plead and manage their own causes personally or by the assistance of..... counsel.....' The right is currently codified in 28 U.S.C. Sec. 1654.
>
> With few exceptions, each of the several States also accords a defendant the right to represent himself in any criminal case. The Constitutions

> of 36 States explicitly confer that right. Moreover, many state courts have expressed the view that the right is also supported by the Constitution of the United States."
>
> 422 U.S. 806.

In Adams v. United States ex rel. McCann, 317 U.S. 260, 270, 87 L Ed 268, 63 S Ct 236, 143 ALR 435, the Supreme Court said:

> "The right to assistance of counsel and the correlative right to dispense with a lawyer's help are not legal formalisms. They rest on considerations that go to the substance of an accused's position before the law....
>
> "....What were contrived as protections for the accused should not be turned into fetters.... To deny an accused a choice of procedure in circumstances in which he, though a layman, is as capable as any lawyer of making an intelligent choice, is to impair the worth of great Constitutional safeguards by treating them as empty verbalisms.
>
> "....When the administration of the criminal law.... is hedged about as it is by the Constitutional safeguards for the protection of an accused, to deny him in the exercise of his free choice the right to dispense with some of these safeguards....is to imprison a man in his privileges and call it the Constitution."

The Faretta case, supra, which settled the issue in criminal cases was summed up by the court's opinion as follows:

> The Sixth and Fourteenth Amendments of our Constitution guarantee that a person brought to trial in any state or federal court must be afforded the right to the assistance of counsel before he can be validly convicted and punished by imprisonment. This clear constitutional rule has emerged from a

> series of cases decided here over the last 50 years. The question before us now is whether a defendant in a state criminal trial has a constitutional right to proceed without counsel when he voluntarily and intelligently elects to do so. Stated another way, the question is whether a State may constitutionally hale a person into its criminal courts and there force a lawyer upon him, even when he insists that he wants to conduct his own defense. It is not an easy question, but we have concluded that a State may not constitutionally do so.
>
> 422 U.S. 806.

Although the Faretta case related specifically to criminal cases, the principle would apply with equal force to civil cases. In an annotation in 67 American Law Reports, Second 1103, it is said:

> "The cases herein are in substantial agreement with the general proposition that a party in a civil action may appear either pro se or through counsel (pursuant to statute in some instances), but that he has no absolute right to do both in the absence of express statutory or constitutional provision."

The Georgia Constitution, Article 1, Section 1, provides:

> "No person shall be deprived of the right to prosecute or defend his own cause in any of the courts of this State, in person, by attorney, or both."

The mere fact that you have a legal right to represent yourself in court does not necessarily mean that you should always dispense with the services of a lawyer.

Fact is, we think there are some well-defined cases in which you must have a lawyer's help to get the protection you need; and there are well defined cases (described herein) where you might be better off without a lawyer. You be the judge!

In the Faretta case one of the three dissenting judges said:

> "If there is any truth to the old proverb that 'one who is his own lawyer has a fool for a client,' the court by its opinion today now bestows a constitutional right on one to make a fool of himself."
>
> 422 U.S. 806.

Another judge said:

> "Pro se representation may at times serve the ideal of a fair trial better than representation by an attorney."
>
> U.S. ex rel Soto v. U.S. (CA 3Pa) 504 F 2d 1339.

The "Standards Relating to Trial Courts" prepared by the American Bar Association Commission on Standards of Judicial Administration, approved by the American Bar Association House of Delegates in February, 1976 provides as follows:

> 2.23 Conduct of Cases Where Litigants Appear Without Counsel. When a litigant undertakes to represent himself, the court should take whatever measures may be reasonable and necessary to insure a fair trial.

COMMENTARY

The duty of the courts to make their procedures fair is not limited to appointing counsel for eligible persons who request representation. In many instances, persons who cannot afford counsel are ineligible for appointed counsel; in other cases, persons who can afford counsel, or who are eligible to be provided with counsel, refuse to be represented. The refusal may be grounded on the litigant's belief that if he has counsel he will be denied any opportunity to speak for himself, that only through personal presentation of his case can he really make known the merits of his case, that no lawyer will faithfully represent him at a fair fee, or that the judicial system is so inherently unjust that his only chance for a fair trial is to represent himself. In other instances, the litigant may believe, reasonably or unreasonably, that the matter in controversy is one in which it is not worth retaining counsel, even though his case is genuinely meritorious and even though the opposing party may have found it in his own interest to retain counsel. In criminal cases, an accused has, at least under some circumstances, a federally guaranteed right to represent himself.

Faretta v. California, 422 U.S. 806 (1975).

All such situations present great difficulties for the court because the court's essential role as an impartial arbiter cannot be performed with the usual confidence that the merits of the case will be fully disclosed through the litigant's presentations. These difficulties are compounded when, as can often be the case, the litigant's capability even as a lay participant appears limited by gross ignorance, inarticulateness, naivete, or mental disorder. They are especially great when one party is represented by counsel and the other is not, for intervention by the court introduces not only ambiguity and potential conflict in the court's role but also consequent ambiguity in the role of counsel for the party who is represented. Yet it is ultimately the judge's responsibility to see that the merits of a controversy are resolved fairly and justly. Fulfilling that responsibility may require that the court, while remaining neutral in consideration of the merits, assume more than a merely passive role in assuring that the merits are adequately presented.

> The proper scope of the court's responsibility is necessarily an expression of careful exercise of judicial discretion and cannot be fully described by specific formula. Legal corollaries of the right to counsel and the experience of conscientious judges establish certain guidelines. Where a litigant is entitled to be provided with assistance of counsel, but indicates a desire to represent himself, the court should fully advise him of his right to representation and the importance of availing himself of it. The court should strongly discourage waiver of counsel and should require the litigant to consult with a lawyer before accepting a waiver of the right. American Bar Association Standards, The Function of the Trial Judge 6.6; Providing Defense Services 7.31. Where the litigant appears primarily interested in an opportunity to state his case personally to the court or jury, he should be assured that he will have reasonable opportunity to speak for himself and may thereby be persuaded to accept the assistance of counsel. In some circumstances it may be appropriate to appoint standby counsel. American Bar Association Standards, The Function of the Trial Judge 6.7. Where a litigant has no right to be provided with counsel, the court in appropriate cases should urge him to retain counsel and facilitate an appropriate referral to the bar for that purpose. Where a litigant represents himself, the court in the interest of fair determination of the merits should ask such questions and suggest the production of such evidence as may be necessary to supplement or clarify the litigant's presentation of the case.

In the final analysis you will have to review the guidelines set out in this book, study your own case carefully (don't hesitate to ask a lawyer his opinion on this question), and make your own decision based on your particular situation. Once you decide to represent yourself -- tear 'em up, Tiger!

One final admonition: don't get the idea that your legal right to handle your own case in court is absolute -- or gets you home free. You must obey all court rules -- and the judge has an almost unlimited discretion in "throwing" you out of court if you don't know how to proceed in an orderly procedure. Follow the instructions given in this book -- and you'll make it!

CHAPTER II

THE TRIAL COURT SYSTEM

A. Federal Courts

The federal courts have jurisdiction in the following:

1. Cases in law and equity arising under the U. S. Constitution, the laws of the United States and treaties -- called "federal question jurisdiction." 28 U.S.C. 1331.

2. Cases affecting ambassadors, counsels, etc;

3. Cases of admiralty and maritime jurisdiction;

4. Cases to which the U. S. is a party;

5. Controversies between two or more states, or between a state and a citizen of another state;

6. Controversies between citizens of different states -- diversity jurisdiction -- or between citizens and foreign nationals. 28 U.S.C. 1332.

B. State Courts

The "subject matter" of state courts varies from state to state, but the general pattern is to have:

1. A trial court of general jurisdiction usually called Superior Court, District Court, Circuit Court,

and others. This is the main trial court in the state.

2. Courts of "limited" jurisdiction -- usually a civil court that handles cases involving amounts up to specified amounts -- ($5,000 to $10,000 is typical). Special probate courts, juvenile courts, domestic relations courts, small claims courts, Justice Courts are examples of other courts of "limited" jurisdiction.

By way of example the trial courts of California are as follows:

1. Superior Court (general jurisdiction): There is one Superior Court in every county of the state, but there are branches in more populous counties. The Superior Court has subject matter jurisdiction as follows:

a. Over all civil litigation in actions at law where the amount demanded (exclusive of interest) or the value of the property in controversy is in excess of $5,000. (One exception: If the county has no municipal court, then the Superior Court's jurisdictional minimum is $500.)

b. General equity jurisdiction, regardless of the amount involved (injunctions, declaratory relief, specific performance, etc.)

c. Exclusive jurisdiction over probate, divorce; and actions involving title to real property or the legality of a tax. California Constitution, Article IV, Section 5, 6.

2. Municipal Court (limited jurisdiction): One in each judicial district created by the state, having a population of 40,000 or more. If less than the requisite population, there is no municipal court. This court has subject matter jurisdiction as follows:

a. Over all actions at law where the amount demanded (exclusive of interest) or the value of the property in controversy is $5,000 or less.

b. In certain equitable actions, for example, to quiet title to personal property valued at $5,000 or less; partnership dissolutions where the assets are $5,000 or less; rescission of contracts if incidental to a claim of $5,000 or less; foreclosure of certain liens where the total claim is $5,000 or less; unlawful detainer actions where the rental value is $600 or less, and the total claim is $5,000 or less.

c. Provided the action is within its original jurisdiction a municipal court may consider any equitable defense; for example, laches, estoppel, etc; may grant temporary restraining orders and injunctions (equitable relief); and may impose liability whether the theory upon which liability is sought to be imposed involves legal or equitable principles.

3. Justice Court: (limited jurisdiction): At least one in every county of the state and one in every judicial district having a population of less than 40,000. A Justice Court has subject matter jurisdiction as follows:

a. Over all actions at law where amount demanded (exclusive of interest) is $1,000 or less.

b. Very limited equitable jurisdiction; for example, to foreclose liens on personal property when lien is $1,000 or less; of unlawful detainer actions where the rental value is $300 or less per month. California Constitution, Article VI, Sections 1, 5, 6, 11. CCP 89, 112.

C. Jurisdiction -- Venue -- Forum Non Conveniens

Essentially "jurisdiction" means two things: (1) Is this the right court to determine this issue (subject matter jurisdiction), and (2) Does the court have the legal power over the parties (in personam jurisdiction).

1. In Personam (personal) Jurisdiction

Where a plaintiff seeks to impose liability upon a defendant (as opposed merely to determining rights of property), or to obtain an order binding the defendant personally, in personam jurisdiction is required.

To subject a person to the jurisdiction of a court there must be proper service of process. This may be done by personal service or by constructive service or substituted service. In all events there is a constitutional requirement of sufficient contact with a jurisdiction to warrant the exercise of jurisdiction over you.

To constitute personal service the process must be served on the defendant while he is physically within the boundaries of the court's jurisdiction. This is the usual way most lawsuits start; but not always. Where a defendant is not in the state or district he may still be served. Constructive service is usually accomplished by publication of copies of the process in newspapers of general circulation, or posting copies in public places. Substituted service is by mailing of process to the defendant at his last known address. This term is also applied where process is personally served on a defendant who is outside the state.

A defendant may voluntarily consent to appear in another jurisdiction, and such appearance is sufficient, but a defendant may also make a "Special Appearance" in most courts to fight jurisdiction. Most states have "long arm statutes" which permit jurisdiction over persons who "transact any business, or commit a tortious act, or breach a contract within the state." The modern trend is for the states to expand the application of these statutes to cover all situations "not inconsistent with the Constitution." Most "long arm statutes" require personal service on the defendant outside the state, or at least, registered mail with return receipt requested. For example, California allows service by any form of airmail requiring a return receipt; or in any manner prescribed by the law of the place where the person is served. CCP 415.10, 40.

2. In Rem Jurisdiction

Where a plaintiff seeks a determination of rights in particular real or personal property, the court need have only in rem jurisdiction -- judicial power over the property -- the "res" -- the thing -- involved. This gives the court power to decide the rights of all persons in the world having any interest in the property -- regardless of whether they are subject to the personal jurisdiction of the court. Typically, this involves title to real or personal property, liens, foreclosures, and the like.

3. Subject Matter Jurisdiction

Subject matter jurisdiction simply relates to whether a particular court, under the statutes and laws, is the right court to decide the particular controversy. For example, you can't go to a probate court to decide "divorce" cases; a "domestic relations" court can't decide probate matters, etc.

The appeal courts of the states usually consist of a supreme court -- or court of appeals (court of last resort) and other appellate courts.

D. Venue

"Venue" refers to the proper place for trial of a lawsuit. In state courts the question usually is which county in the state is the proper place for trial; in federal courts -- which judicial district.

Statutes regulating venue vary from state to state. In general, the codes provide that the proper court for trial of "transitory" actions is in the county in which any defendant resides. Special statutes frequently make other counties also proper for trial of certain kinds of cases; for example, personal injury cases in the county where the accident occurs; contract actions in the county where the contract was entered into or to be performed.

The venue for "local" actions is always the county where the property is located. And in a few states the policy that litigation involving local land be heard locally is so strong that venue is deemed a jurisdictional requirement as to certain kinds of actions; that is, that the action must be commenced there.

Proceedings to change venue are costly and often cause a delay in bringing the matter to trial. For this reason, some state codes authorize the court to award reasonable expenses and attorney's fees to the prevailing party in such proceedings. Some statutes also stipulate that the expenses and fees must be paid by the attorney for the losing party in the venue proceedings out of his own pocket. This is an obvious over-reaction to the practice of lawyers taking such measures to "delay" cases.

CHAPTER III
RULES OF COURT

IN GENERAL

In defending yourself in any court action the first thing you must have is a copy of the court rules -- the general court rules -- and a copy of any "local" court rules. In the federal courts the general court rules are called Federal Rules of Civil Procedure. Most Federal District Courts have a separate set of local rules which you must follow -- to stay in court!

In state courts the general court rules are called by various names including Rules of Court, Rules of Civil Procedure, Courts and Proceedings in Civil Cases, Rules, Civil Practice and Procedure, Courts and Civil Procedure, Rules of Procedure, and other similar name tags.

Each state has these rules in its statute books or special rule books or both. They are easy to find in any law library. The Federal rules are used as a model or pattern for the state rules, therefore we will review in principle the federal rules to discuss the most important items you need to know. The federal rules were recently liberalized in certain "discovery" procedures, therefore we will use typical state rules in discussing discovery procedures. Many of the states have the same numbering system as the federal rules -- but not all. The few differences -- or variations -- will be mentioned, but you must, in all events, get a copy of your own court rules if you have, or will have, a pending case.

Every application to the court for an order must be made by motion or petition which should be in writing unless made during a hearing or trial. The written motion serves as notice to one's adversary and also serves the function of preserving a written record of the proceedings.

The basic parts of pleadings are:

1. Caption (court, file number, parties names)
2. Introductory clause (what the pleading is)
3. Body (allegations)
4. Demand for judgment or other relief (what you want)
5. Signature (by attorney or the individual party)
6. Certificate of service (except complaint and summons). A certificate of service is not appropriate on a complaint or other original papers because they have to be served on the defendant.

Most court rules start with the pronouncement in Rule 1 that the purpose of the rules is to effect "the just, speedy and inexpensive determination of litigation."

Basically a "civil action" is to resolve a controversy between parties and the purpose of pleadings is to develop the material issues of law and fact upon which to resolve the controversy.

Motions need not necessarily be on a separate piece of paper; you can put several in one document. You need to send a copy of all pleadings to the other parties and the typical certificate of service is:

I hereby certify that a copy hereof has been furnished to __(party or his lawyer)__ by (delivery, mail) this ____ day of __________.

(Your signature).

Some local rules require the filing of written briefs or authorities upon which the party relies. This can be very short. Do not argue in your motions -- argue like hell in your legal briefs. If it is necessary to verify a pleading the usual form is:

Before me, the undersigned authority, this day personally appeared ________________________, who was sworn and says: ____.

Sworn to and subscribed before me on the ____ day of __________.

(Seal -- Signed by Notary)

In some state courts the pleadings allowed are:

Plaintiff's Pleadings	Defendant's Pleadings
Complaint	Demurrer Answer
Demurrer to Answer	Cross-complaint
Demurrer to Cross-complaint	
Answer to Cross-complaint	Demurrer to Answer to Cross-complaint

Pleadings under federal rules and most state rules include:

Plaintiff's Pleadings	Defendant's Pleadings
Complaint	Answer which may contain either counterclaim against plaintiff or cross-claim against co-defendant
Reply to Counterclaim	
Answer to Cross-claim	Third Party Complaint

Offensive pleadings are those which set forth a claim for relief; defensive pleadings are statements of defenses. Complaint is a claim asserted by a plaintiff against a defendant; counter-claim is a claim asserted by a defendant against a plaintiff. Cross-claim is a claim by a defendant against a co-defendant or other party in the action. Third Party Complaint is a claim asserted by a defendant against one who is not a party to the original action which is, or may be, liable to the defendant for all or a part of the plaintiff's claim against defendant.

Most court rules provide that a pleading which sets forth a claim for relief, whether an original claim, counterclaim, cross-claim, or third party claim, shall contain (1) a short and plain statement of the grounds upon which the court's jurisdiction depends, (2) a short and plain statement of the claim showing that the pleader is entitled to relief, and (3) a demand for judgment for the relief to which he deems himself entitled. Relief in the alternative or of several different types may be demanded. Averments shall be simple, concise, and direct. All pleadings shall be so construed as to do substantial justice.

Averments in a pleading to which a responsive pleading is required, other than those as to the amount of damage, are admitted when not denied in the responsive pleading. Averments in a pleading to which no responsive pleading is required or permitted shall be taken as denied or avoided.

The pleadings prescribed in the court rules are merely one stage in the issue-narrowing process; discovery devices and pre-trial conferences are also available. The modern trend in all court rules is to liberalize the rules of pleading and streamline the pleading process so as to assure a determination of the litigation promptly and on the merits. At least, this is what the rule makers say.

WHAT IS A CAUSE OF ACTION?

A cause of action is generally defined as the fact or facts which establish or give rise to a right of action, the existence of which affords a party a right to judicial relief. It is the right a party has to institute a judicial proceeding. A cause of action is that single group of facts which is claimed to have brought about an unlawful injury to the plaintiff and which entitles him to relief.

In common parlance a cause of action is frequently referred to as action, suit, cause, proceeding, lawsuit or a right "to sue the bastards." Under the modern court rules technical forms of action or technical remedies have been abolished and in most states there is but one form of action in civil suits, known as "civil action."

A right of action, or the plaintiff's right to sue, is determined or affected by three considerations: (1) There must be a cause of action; (2) all conditions precedent to bringing the suit must be performed, and (3) there must not be a defense or bar to the maintenance of the suit.

The textbooks state it this way: The essential elements of a good cause of action are the existence of a legal right in the plaintiff, with a corresponding legal duty in the defendant, and a violation or breach of that right or duty, with consequential injury or damage to the plaintiff, for which he may maintain an action for recovery of money damages, or other appropriate relief.

FORMS

The forms listed in this book are for illustration only, however when used along with the form books cited in the Appendix, you will be able to take care of all your needs. The heading on Form 1 is an example only and you should check with the clerk of your court where your case is pending to get the style and format for the heading on your pleadings. Most court rules provide that in the caption of the summons and in the caption of the complaint all parties must be named but in other pleadings and papers, it is sufficient to state the name of the first party on either side, with an appropriate indication of other parties. For example, John Doe, et al, v. ABC Corp, et al.

Some courts require a jurisdictional allegation; some do not. Check your statutes and check with your court clerk.

Each pleading, motion, and other paper should be signed by at least one attorney of record, in his individual name, with his address and telephone number. If a party is not represented by an attorney, the signature, address and telephone number of the party (pro se) should be used. In all events the name and address of the plaintiff should be shown on the complaint and the name and address of the defendant should be shown on the answer. This is to furnish a proper address for service if appeal is later filed.

The complaint in Form 3 has more counts than the average lawsuit, but these are included to give you more examples. The names, addresses and facts are wholly hypothetical and fictitious, and are used for illustration only.

Your court rules will probably have examples of forms to be used in your court. Be sure to review your own rules and forms before filing your pleadings.

A. Commencement of Action: Complaint and Summons

Rule 3: A civil action is commenced by filing a complaint with the court.

The pleading must set forth the name of the court, the number assigned to the action, the designation of the pleading (complaint for damages, motion to dismiss, etc.), and the name of the parties.

Rule 4: Process

This rule provides that upon the filing of a complaint the clerk shall forthwith issue a summons. It specifies that service of process shall be made by a United States Marshal, by his deputy, or by some person specially appointed by the court for that purpose. Most state courts permit the sheriff, deputy sheriff or any adult not interested in the suit to serve process. Generally personal service is made by delivery of the summons and complaint to the defendant personally, or by leaving copies thereof at his dwelling house or usual place of abode with some person of suitable age and discretion then residing therein or by delivering a copy of the summons and of the complaint to an agent authorized by appointment or by law to receive service of process.

There are specific methods for service of process on corporations, partnerships, associations, the government, a party not an inhabitant of, or found within, the state, and others.

Constitutional due process of law (14th Amendment) requires various standards in giving notice and an opportunity to defend. In some state courts the action is commenced by the service of a summons before the complaint is filed.

Rule 5: Service and Filing of Pleadings and other papers.

The general practice in most courts is to require that the original copy of a pleading (and sometimes one carbon copy) be filed with the court clerk, and that one copy be sent to each party to the action. Be sure to check your local rules because they frequently require that a supporting brief or memorandum of law be filed to support your motions.

Rule 6: Time

The usual provision for computing any period of time prescribed or allowed by the rules, is that the day of the act, event, or default from which the designated period of time begins to run shall not be included. The last day of the period so computed shall be included, unless it is a Saturday, a Sunday, or a legal holiday, in which event the period runs until the end of the next day which is not a Saturday, a Sunday, or a legal holiday. Legal holidays generally include New Years Day, Washington's Birthday, Memorial Day, Independence Day, Labor Day, Columbus Day, Veteran's Day, Thanksgiving Day, Christmas Day.

The court may, of course, upon timely motion enlarge the time periods set out in the rules. This is an easy way to delay any proceeding -- if you have a good reason to ask for an extension of time to file. Most judges will routinely grant your first request. Lawyers ask all the time. Moreover, most lawyers will voluntarily agree to extensions for almost any -- or no -- reason. After all why should they be in a hurry? If you get friendly with the plaintiff's lawyer, you can probably delay him -- voluntarily -- for years.

Form 1: Summons

IN THE UNITED STATES DISTRICT COURT

IN AND FOR THE SOUTHERN

DISTRICT OF CALIFORNIA

Civil Action Number ____

Black Jack, Plaintiff	)	
	)	
v.	)	SUMMONS
	)	
John Good, Defendant	)	

You are hereby summoned and required to serve upon ______, plaintiff's attorney, whose address is _________, an answer to the complaint which is herewith served upon you, within ____ days after service of this summons upon you, exclusive of the day of service. If you fail to do so, judgment by default will be taken against you for the relief demanded in the complaint.

Seal of Court

Date:_____________

____
Clerk of Court

Form 2: Allegations of Jurisdiction

a. Jurisdiction founded on diversity of citizenship and amount -- Federal Court

IN THE UNITED STATES DISTRICT COURT

IN AND FOR THE SOUTHERN

DISTRICT OF CALIFORNIA

Civil Action Number ____

Black Jack, Plaintiff, v. John Good, Defendant	)))))))	COMPLAINT

Plaintiff is a citizen of the State of A and defendant is a corporation, incorporated under the laws of the State of B -- having its principal place of business in a State other than the State of A. The matter in controversy exceeds, exclusive of interest and costs, the sum of ten thousand dollars.

Seal of Court ____________________ Clerk of Court

Date: ____________________

Form 2: Allegations of Jurisdiction

b. Jurisdiction founded on the existence of a Federal Question -- Federal Court

IN THE DISTRICT COURT

IN AND FOR ANYWHERE COUNTY

STATE OF ANYWHERE

Civil Action Number ____

Black Jack, Plaintiff,	)	
	)	
v.	)	COMPLAINT
	)	
John Good, Defendant	)	

This action arises under the Fourteenth Amendment of the U. S. Constitution, Section 1, and 42 U.S.C. 1983, as hereafter more fully appears. The matter in controversy exceeds, exclusive of interest and costs, the sum of ten thousand dollars.

Seal of Court

Date:____________

____
Clerk of Court

Form 2: Allegations of Jurisdiction

c. Jurisdiction allegations in state courts of limited jurisdiction

IN THE DISTRICT COURT

IN AND FOR ANYWHERE COUNTY

STATE OF ANYWHERE

Civil Action Number ____

Black Jack, Plaintiff,	)	
v.	)	COMPLAINT
John Good, Defendant	)	

This action is based on a claim which does not exceed the sum of five thousand dollars, and is within the jurisdictional limits of this court.

Seal of Court

____
Clerk of Court

Date: ____________

Form 3: Complaint

IN THE DISTRICT COURT

IN AND FOR ANYWHERE COUNTY

STATE OF ANYWHERE

Civil Action Number ____

Black Jack, Plaintiff,	)))	
v.	)	COMPLAINT
John Good, Defendant	)))	

COUNT I (Promissory Note)

1. Defendant on or about July 1, 1976, executed and delivered to plaintiff a promissory note, copy of which is attached hereto as Exhibit A, whereby defendant promised to pay to plaintiff or order on July 1, 1977, the sum of $1000 with interest thereon at the rate of 10 percent per annum.

2. Defendant owes to plaintiff the amount of said note and interest plus attorney's fees.

Wherefore plaintiff demands judgment against defendant for the sum of $1000 plus interest, court costs, expenses, and attorney's fees.

Form 3: Complaint (continued)

COUNT II (Account)

3. Defendant owes plaintiff $1000 according to the account attached hereto as Exhibit B.

Wherefore plaintiff demands judgment against defendant for the sum of $1000 plus interest, court costs, expenses, and attorney's fees.

COUNT III (Negligence)

4. On July 1, 1976, on a public highway called First Street in City, State, defendant negligently drove a motor vehicle against plaintiff who was then crossing said highway.

5. As a result plaintiff was thrown down and had his leg broken and was otherwise injured, was prevented from transacting his business, suffered great pain of body and mind, and incurred expenses for medical attention and hospitalization in the sum of $1000.

Wherefore plaintiff demands judgment against defendant in the sum of $50,000 plus interests, court costs, expenses and attorney's fees.

Black Jack
123 First Street
City, State
300-333-3434
In Pro Per

B. Attacking the Complaint

Before filing an answer to the complaint the defendant may challenge the legal sufficiency of the complaint -- why not? It takes a long time! There is a full arsenal of pleadings you can use to run the plaintiff and his attorney ragged! Lawyers frequently refer to these motions as "Rule 12 motions." Everybody around the courthouse knows what that term means! Delay.

Rule 12. Defenses and Objections — When and How Presented — By Pleading or Motion — Motion for Judgment on Pleadings

(a) When Presented. A defendant shall serve his answer within 20 days after the service of the summons and complaint upon him, except when service is made under Rule 4(e) and a different time is prescribed in the order of court under the statute of the United States or in the statute or rule of court of the state. A party served with a pleading stating a cross-claim against him shall serve an answer thereto within 20 days after the service upon him. The plaintiff shall serve his reply to a counterclaim in the answer within 20 days after service of the answer or, if a reply is ordered by the court, within 20 days after service of the order, unless the order otherwise directs. The United States or an officer or agency thereof shall serve an answer to the complaint or to a cross-claim, or a reply to a counterclaim, within 60 days after the service upon the United States attorney of the pleading in which the claim is asserted. The service of a motion permitted under this rule alters these periods of time as follows, unless a different time is fixed by order of the court: (1) if the court denies the motion or postpones its disposition until the trial on the merits, the responsive pleading shall be served within 10 days after notice of the court's action; (2) if the court grants a motion for a more definite statement the responsive pleading shall be served within 10 days after the service of the more definite statement.

(b) How Presented. Every defense, in law or fact, to a claim for relief in any pleading, whether a claim, counterclaim, cross-claim, or third-party claim, shall be asserted in the responsive pleading thereto if one is required, except that the following defenses may at the option of the pleader be made by motion: (1) lack of jurisdiction over the subject matter, (2) lack of jurisdiction over the person, (3) improper venue, (4) insufficiency of process, (5) insufficiency of service of process, (6) failure to state a claim upon which relief can be granted, (7) failure to join a party under Rule 19. A motion making any of these defenses shall be made before pleading if a further pleading is permitted. No defense or objection is waived by being joined with one or more other defenses or objections in a responsive pleading or motion. If a pleading sets forth a claim for relief to which the adverse party is not required to serve a responsive pleading, he may assert at the trial any defense in law or fact to that claim for relief. If, on a motion asserting the defense numbered (6) to dismiss for failure of the pleading to state a claim upon which relief can be granted, matters outside the pleading are presented to and not excluded by the court, the motion shall be treated as one for summary judgment and disposed of as provided in Rule 56, and all parties shall be given reasonable opportunity to present all material made pertinent to such a motion by Rule 56.

(c) Motion for Judgment on the Pleadings. After the pleadings are closed but within such time as not to delay the trial, any party may move for judgment on the pleadings. If, on a motion for judgment on the pleadings, matters outside the pleadings are presented to and not excluded by the court, the motion shall be treated as one for summary judgment and disposed of as provided in Rule 56, and all parties shall be given reasonable opportunity to present all material made pertinent to such a motion by Rule 56.

(d) Preliminary Hearings. The defenses specifically enumerated (1)-(7) in subdivision (b) of this rule, whether made in a pleading or by motion, and the motion for judgment mentioned in subdivision (c) of this rule shall be heard and determined before trial on application of any party, unless the court orders that the hearing and determination thereof be deferred until the trial.

(e) Motion for More Definite Statement. If a pleading to which a responsive pleading is permitted is so vague or ambiguous that a party cannot reasonably be required to frame a responsive pleading. The motion shall point out the defects complained of and the details desired. If the motion is granted and the order of the court is not obeyed within 10 days after notice of the order or within such other time as the court may fix, the court may strike the pleading to which the motion was directed or make such order as it deems just.

(f) Motion to Strike. Upon motion made by a party before responding to a pleading or, if no responsive pleading is permitted by these rules, upon motion made by a party within 20 days after the service of the pleading upon him or upon the court's own initiative at any time, the court may order stricken from any pleading any insufficient defense or any redundant, immaterial, impertinent, or scandalous matter.

(g) Consolidation of Defenses in Motion. A party who makes a motion under this rule may join with it any other motions herein provided for and then available to him. If a party makes a motion under this rule but omits therefrom any defense or objection then available to him which this rule permits to be raised by motion, he shall not thereafter make a motion based on the defense or objection so omitted, except a motion as provided in subdivision (h)(2) hereof on any of the grounds there stated.

(h) Waiver or Preservation of Certain Defenses.

(1) A defense of lack of jurisdiction over the person, improper venue, insufficiency of process, or insufficiency of service of process is waived (A) if omitted from a motion in the circumstances described in subdivision (g), or (B) if it is neither made by motion under this rule nor included in a responsive pleading or an amendment thereof permitted by Rule 15(a) to be made as a matter of course.

(2) A defense of failure to state a claim upon which relief can be granted, a defense of failure

> to join a party indispensable under Rule 19, and an objection of failure to state a legal defense to a claim may be made in any pleading permitted or ordered under Rule 7(a), or by motion for judgment on the pleadings, or at the trial on the merits.
> (3) Whenever it appears by suggestion of the parties or otherwise that the court lacks jurisdiction of the subject matter, the court shall dismiss the action.

Where a defendant files a motion "permitted under this rule" it alters the period of time for filing your answer! And who's in a hurry? Let's talk about these "Rule 12 Motions." They are more fun than a toy pistol and more effective than a double barreled shotgun.

1. Motion To Dismiss: This motion may be called a "demurrer" in some state rules. It is the same thing. In testing the sufficiency of a complaint under Rule 12 motions the court will construe it in the light most favorable to the plaintiff. The plaintiff need only state a claim upon which relief may be granted -- he need not state facts about his evidence. The sufficiency of the complaint is determined from the facts pleaded and reasonable inferences to be drawn from them.

If you attack the lack of jurisdiction, insufficiency of process or service of process you may need to file an affidavit to give the judge evidence to support your point. For example, if the deputy sheriff left the summons and complaint with your neighbor instead of you or your family, you should file an affidavit to prove your facts to the judge.

If the judge grants your motion to dismiss for failure to state a cause of action he will always let the plaintiff amend at least one time -- and usually more. Of course, this takes a lot of time. If your motion is denied you then proceed to file your answer, but only after all Rule 12 motions have been ruled on by the court.

2. Motion For More Definite Statement: This is called a Bill of Particulars in some states. Because of the liberal construction of the "simple" statement rule most courts won't grant this motion -- but most complaints are vague or ambiguous. And this always gives you a good shot at convincing the judge to grant your motion. As a safety measure you should flood the plaintiff with a load of written interrogatories about the facts alleged in his complaint -- and you generally get his answers under oath long before you ever have to file your answer to the complaint. And remember, when you file this motion don't bother to call it up for hearing, unless the rules require it. Maybe it will just sit there forever.

3. Motion To Strike: Either party may move to strike any insufficient defense or any "redundant, immaterial,

impertinent or scandalous" matter in the pleadings of the other party. Most judges don't like these motions, but if the other party gets a little nasty in his allegations give him a shot. Profane or repulsive language is generally improper in a pleading. Moreover, in some courts a party is permitted to read the pleadings to the jury at the trial. In those courts you should flood them with Motions to Strike. But remember, you can also read the other guy's pleadings to the jury if you want to!

4. Procedure: Rule 12 motions must be in writing (See Rule 7.) and must specify the ground or grounds upon which they are based. In other words tell the judge the reasons you are relying on. Always file the motions within the 20 or 30 days stated in the summons; and check your local rules about filing briefs.

5. Waiver: When you file a Rule 12 motion include all defenses permitted and also file all of the motions you plan to use under Rule 12 otherwise they are waived; except the following basic defenses are never waived and can be raised at any time: lack of jurisdiction over subject matter, failure to join an indispensible party, and failure to state a claim upon which relief can be granted (or failure to state a cause of action).

6. How To Get A Hearing On Your Motions: The local procedures vary as to how a party arranges to have his motions ruled on by the judge. In some courts the judge may rule without a hearing. In most courts one of the parties has to check with the clerk, the judge's secretary, the judge's clerk, or some other court official to arrange for a hearing. Check your local rules. In some courts there is an old-fashioned procedure to file a formal "notice" of a time to appear in court to get an appointment. Of course, when you file a Rule 12 motion -- unless the local rules require it -- you do not have to arrange to call them up for hearing. In other words where the rules do not require it (and most do not) you can just let the motion sit there -- forever -- and unless the attorney for the plaintiff arranges for a hearing, you can let it stay in status quo 'til hell freezes over! I have seen many lawsuits dismissed for lack of prosecution where neither party (or the lawyers) bothered to schedule a hearing on pending motions. Moreover, I have seen many lawyers let a case hang in suspension -- while telling their clients, "I can't do anything until the judge rules on the pending motions." Little did the client know he had a lazy -- or stupid -- lawyer. I have also prosecuted many "disciplinary" proceedings (for the bar association) and presided over such disciplinary proceedings (as a member of ethics committees) where lawyers failed to arrange

for hearings on pending motions -- and told the client he was waiting for "the judge" to act! The burden of what I am saying is that you will find <u>many</u> lawyers who will let motions hang forever -- let's say they are "too busy" to arrange for hearings.

Another Tip: Here's one I have seen pulled off many times -- especially on young, inexperienced lawyers. Arrange for a hearing on your motions; a day or two before the hearing date call the judge's secretary or clerk and cancel -- or postpone -- the hearing. Reschedule it maybe two months later. Once I heard this story: A young hot-headed lawyer represented the owner of a mortgage on a small house owned and occupied by a young client and his family. A major dispute -- well, maybe a minor dispute -- developed around Christmas time one year (and the client didn't have any money and could not make the mortgage payments). The client stalled a foreclosure on the mortgage for several months without making any payments. Finally, on April 14, the lawyer filed the foreclosure and was very anxious to kick the client out. The client's lawyer on the 30th day filed a series of Rule 12 motions and a set of written interrogatories and requests for admission of facts. He called the judge's secretary and learned the judge planned to go on his summer vacation (trip to Europe) on June 21. He scheduled a hearing on the motions for June 14 -- knowing the judge would be swamped with hearings the last week on the bench before his vacation, and sent a "notice" of hearing to the other lawyer. On June 10 he called the judge's secretary, cancelled the June 14th hearing date, and wrote the young lawyer a letter telling him the hearing had been cancelled, that he was leaving for a vacation and the judge had no time available during the next week for another hearing date -- and just dropped it there! The plaintiff's hot-headed lawyer wasn't able to get a hearing date until September. The client was able to make the payments long before the judge got back from his summer vacation!

Get on good terms with the court personnel and you can discover many advantages in handling your own case -- and a million ways to delay. They have seen all of them!

C. Answer and Defenses

Your answer tells the plaintiff what you deny in his complaint, and what "goodies" you have lined up for him by way of defenses -- or alleged defenses. It is good practice for you to respond separately to the numbered paragraphs of the complaint and unequivocally deny or admit. If you don't deny some allegations they may be deemed admitted. It is generally poor and sloppy practice to deny everything (general denial) in the complaint -- it can't be that bad -- can it? It is good practice to admit truthful allegations that are easy to prove. Like

(continued on page 3-33)

Form 4: Motion to Dismiss

IN THE DISTRICT COURT

IN AND FOR ANYWHERE COUNTY

STATE OF ANYWHERE

Civil Action Number ____

Black Jack, Plaintiff,	)))	
v.	))	MOTION TO DISMISS
John Good, Defendant	))	

Defendant moves for the entry of an order dismissing the complaint on the following grounds:

1. The complaint fails to state a claim against defendant upon which relief can be granted in that: (here insert the specific grounds on which the court should dismiss the action).

2. Lack of jurisdiction over the subject matter in that ________________(state grounds).

3. Lack of jurisdiction over the person in that ______________________.

4. Insufficiency of process in that ______________.

5. Insufficiency of service of process in that ______________________.

Form 4: Motion to Dismiss (continued)

6. Failure to join an indispensible party, it affirmatively appearing from the allegations of the complaint that ___________________ (state specific grounds).

I hereby certify that a copy hereof was mailed to __________________ on the ____ day of ______________.

Your Name
Address
Phone Number
In Pro Per

Form 5: Motion To Strike

IN THE DISTRICT COURT

IN AND FOR ANYWHERE COUNTY

STATE OF ANYWHERE

Civil Action Number ____

Black Jack, Plaintiff, v. John Good, Defendant	)))))))	MOTION TO STRIKE

Defendant moves for the entry of an order striking the following parts of the complaint on the grounds that they are redundant, immaterial, impertinent and scandalous:

1.

2.

3.

(Certificate of Service) (Signature)

Form 6: Motion For More Definite Statement

IN THE DISTRICT COURT

IN AND FOR ANYWHERE COUNTY

STATE OF ANYWHERE

Civil Action Number ____

Black Jack, Plaintiff,	)))	MOTION FOR MORE
v.	))	DEFINITE STATEMENT
John Good, Defendant	))	

Defendant moves for a more definite statement of the following:

1.

2.

because each of them is so vague and ambiguous that defendant cannot reasonably frame a responsive pleading.

(Certificate of Service) (Signature)

Form 7: Motion For Judgment On Pleadings

IN THE DISTRICT COURT

IN AND FOR ANYWHERE COUNTY

STATE OF ANYWHERE

Civil Action Number ____

Black Jack, Plaintiff, v. John Good, Defendant	)))))))	MOTION FOR JUDGMENT ON PLEADINGS

Defendant moves for a judgment on the pleadings.

(Certificate of Service) (Signature)

Form 8: Notice of Hearing

IN THE DISTRICT COURT

IN AND FOR ANYWHERE COUNTY

STATE OF ANYWHERE

Civil Action Number ____

Black Jack, Plaintiff,	)))	
v.	)	NOTICE OF HEARING
John Good, Defendant	)))	

Notice is hereby given that defendant will call up for hearing the Motion To Dismiss before the Honorable Roy Bean in his chambers in the Royal County Courthouse, 888 First Street, City, State on the 14th day of June, 1977, at 9 A.M. or as soon thereafter as the parties may be heard.

(Certificate of Service) (Signature)

Form 9: Order Granting Motion To Dismiss

IN THE DISTRICT COURT

IN AND FOR ANYWHERE COUNTY

STATE OF ANYWHERE

Civil Action Number ___

Black Jack, Plaintiff,	)))	ORDER GRANTING
v.	))	MOTION TO DISMISS
John Good, Defendant	))	

This action was heard on defendant's motion to dismiss the complaint, and it is

ADJUDGED as follows:

1. The complaint is dismissed.

2. Plaintiff shall have 20 days from this date within which to file and serve an Amended Complaint, and defendant shall have 20 days after service of the Amended Complaint within which to respond.

Done and Ordered this ____ day of June, 1977, at City, State.

____
Judge

"plaintiff is over the age of 21 ......" You'd probably admit that, yes? Moreover, the rules require good faith pleadings. But ambiguous, uncertain, or vague allegations shouldn't slip by you, especially if they are hard for the plaintiff to prove. And you don't have to admit essential elements of plaintiff's cause of action that are couched in conclusions -- he has to prove it! For example, here's a story (true) I like to tell about my wife: she got a traffic ticket for failure to stop at a stop sign. She didn't stop! I went to court with her and when the judge said, "How do you plead?" I said, "Not Guilty." My wife looked up at me, surprised, and said, "But that's lying, isn't it?" I had to explain to her that under the laws and constitutions a person doesn't have to convict himself -- the prosecutor has to prove it. Same with civil litigation. If plaintiff alleged I owed him $100 and I file an answer and "admit" it, he is automatically entitled to a judgment. Your testimony under oath about "facts" is a different matter, but you can damn sure deny conclusions alleged in plaintiff's complaint. For example, you may "admit" you borrowed $100 from plaintiff, but "deny" you owe him $100. Who knows how many defenses you may "discover" in your court proceedings. In all events you can put a plaintiff to his proof.

After responding separately -- and carefully -- to the allegations of the complaint you should then affirmatively state any of the specific defenses you <u>may</u> have -- or be entitled to assert -- under Rule 8 -- or otherwise.

Affirmative defenses involve "new matter" which must be pleaded in the answer -- and proven at trial -- to avoid the plaintiff's claim. You may waive your defenses if you don't plead them in your answer. You always have the burden of proof on these issues. For example, you may admit you owed the plaintiff $1000 (once upon a time), but plead that the statute of limitations is a bar to the action. If the statute of limitations has run on the claim he can't collect a dime from you. And look at all the other "possible" defenses listed below.

In order to emphasize the importance of the affirmative defenses listed in most of the court rules, they are reported here for your convenience:

Accord and Satisfaction
Arbitration and Award
Assumption of Risk
Contributory Negligence
Discharge in Bankruptcy
Duress
Estoppel
Failure of Consideration
Fraud
Illegality
Injury by Fellow Servant
Laches
License
Payment
Release
Res Judicata
Statute of Frauds
Statute of Limitations
Waiver
Others (See definitions in Glossary)

Form 10: Answer

IN THE DISTRICT COURT

IN AND FOR ANYWHERE COUNTY

STATE OF ANYWHERE

Civil Action Number ____

Black Jack, Plaintiff,	)))	
v.	)	ANSWER
John Good, Defendant	)))	

Defendant answers the complaint as follows:

1. Defendant denies the allegations of paragraph 1.

2. Defendant admits the allegations of paragraph 2.

3. Defendant admits he signed a promissory note as alleged in the complaint but denies that he owes the plaintiff any sum whatsoever as is more specifically alleged hereafter.

4. Defendant is without sufficient knowledge or information to form a belief of the allegations of paragraph 4 of the complaint and therefore denies the same.

FIRST DEFENSE

5. The complaint fails to state a claim upon which relief may be granted.

Form 10: Answer (continued)

SECOND DEFENSE (Statute of Frauds)

6. The purported contract set forth in plaintiff's complaint by which defendant is sought to be charged is not in writing and signed by defendant or by some person authorized by defendant, as required by ________ (cite statute). Furthermore, there is no note or memorandum of the alleged contract subscribed by defendant or by his agent, as required by said statute.

THIRD DEFENSE (Accord and Satisfaction)

7. On or about July 4, 1977, an agreement was reached between defendant and plaintiff that in satisfaction of any and all claims that plaintiff might have against defendant at the date thereof defendant should pay to the plaintiff the sum of $500 in full satisfaction of any and all claims of plaintiff against defendant as aforesaid, even though defendant at the time of making the said agreement and payment disputed and denied the claim of plaintiff, it being defendant's contention that __________ (state contentions). Therefore, defendant does not owe plaintiff any money whatsoever.

Form 10: Answer (continued)

FOURTH DEFENSE (Duress)

8. The instrument sued on herein was obtained from defendant by plaintiff by duress of defendant sufficient to deny defendant the exercise of his free will, when plaintiff, on the 28th day of June, 1976, at City, State, threatened defendant with ___________ (state specific threats) under the following circumstances:___________. Defendant, fearful and apprehensive of the possible consequences of the act threatened by plaintiff, executed and delivered the instrument solely as a result of plaintiff's threats, and for no other reason.

FIFTH DEFENSE (Statute of Limitations)

9. This action was not commenced within _____ years after the cause of action accrued; consequently, it is barred by the applicable statute of limitation of this state (cite statute).

Wherefore, defendant having fully answered the complaint demands that the same be dismissed and defendant be awarded his cost, expenses and attorney's fees.

(Certificate of Service) (Signature)

If, when you file your answer, you are uncertain about whether you have evidence or facts to support a defense plead it anyway. Find the evidence later. Don't lose a good defense by failing to assert it in your answer. Who knows you may find some evidence to support them! Like "duress," "fraud," and the like. At least you can ask the plaintiff about it in written interrogatories. And who's in a hurry?

D. Counterclaims and Cross-Claims

> Rule 13. Counterclaim and Cross-Claim
>
> (a) Compulsory Counterclaims. A pleading shall state as a counterclaim any claim which at the time of serving the pleading the pleader has against any opposing party, if it arises out of the transaction or occurrence that is the subject matter of the opposing party's claim and does not require for its adjudication the presence of third parties of whom the court cannot acquire jurisdiction. But the pleader need not state the claim if (1) at the time the action was commenced the claim was the subject of another pending action, or (2) the opposing party brought suit upon his claim by attachment or other process by which the court did not acquire jurisdiction to render a personal judgment on that claim, and the pleader is not stating any counterclaim under this Rule 13.
>
> (b) Permissive Counterclaims. A pleading may state as a counterclaim any claim against an opposing party not arising out of the transaction or occurrence that is the subject matter of the opposing party's claim.
>
> (c) Counterclaim Exceeding Opposing Claim. A counterclaim may or may not diminish or defeat the recovery sought by the opposing party. It may

claim relief exceeding in amount or different in kind from that sought in the pleading of the opposing party.

(d) Counterclaim Against the United States. These rules shall not be construed to enlarge beyond the limits now fixed by law the right to assert counterclaims or to claim credits against the United States or an officer or agency thereof.

(e) Counterclaim Maturing or Acquired After Pleading. A claim which either matured or was acquired by the pleader after serving his pleading may, with the permission of the court, be presented as a counterclaim by supplemental pleading.

(f) Omitted Counterclaim. When a pleader fails to set up a counterclaim through oversight, inadvertence, or excusable neglect, or when justice requires, he may by leave of court set up the counterclaim by amendment.

(g) Cross-Claim Against Co-Party. A pleading may state as a cross-claim any claim by one party against a co-party arising out of the transaction or occurrence that is the subject matter either of the original action or of a counterclaim therein or relating to any property that is the subject matter of the original action. Such cross-claim may include a claim that the party against whom it is asserted is or may be liable to the cross-claimant for all or part of a claim asserted in the action against the cross-claimant.

(h) Joinder of Additional Parties. Persons other than those made parties to the original action may be made parties to a counterclaim or cross-claim in accordance with the provisions of Rules 10 and 20.

(i) Separate Trials; Separate Judgments. If the court orders separate trials as provided in Rule 42(b), judgment on a counterclaim or cross-claim may be rendered in accordance with the terms of Rule 54(b) when the court has jurisdiction so to do, even if the claims of the opposing party have been dismissed or otherwise disposed of.

You file your Rule 12 motions. That takes a lot of time to get them resolved. You file your answer with any affirmative defenses you may have. During this time you have been pounding away at the plaintiff with written interrogatories, requests for admission of facts, motions to produce, etc. You are not finished yet! As long as you have to be in court anyway you might as well sue that "turkey" plaintiff for all he owes you. Your counterclaim may be related to the claims set forth in the complaint (compulsory), but it need not be. If your claim arises out of the same transaction or occurrence as that alleged in the complaint it is compulsory -- you must file it now or lose it. If your claim is based on some independent ground (anything at all) it is permissive -- you can counterclaim now -- or sue the bastard later -- at your option. But as long as you are there -- why not give it a shot?

Now, after you consider your lawsuits against the plaintiff you should consider suing any other parties in the case -- any co-defendants or co-plaintiffs. This is done by a cross-claim -- in the same suit. However, your cross-claim against a co-defendant must relate to the "transaction or occurrence" alleged in the complaint. Your answer, counterclaim and cross-claim can all be in the same pleading in most courts.

Form 11: Counterclaim

IN THE DISTRICT COURT

IN AND FOR ANYWHERE COUNTY

STATE OF ANYWHERE

Civil Action Number ____

Black Jack, Plaintiff,	)))	
v.	)	COUNTERCLAIM
John Good, Defendant	)))	

Defendant, Counterclaimant, sues the plaintiff, counter-defendant and alleges:

1. That on the 1st day of June, 1976, counterclaimant bargained with counter-defendant for the purchase of a horse belonging to counter-defendant and that the counter-defendant, to induce counterclaimant to buy the horse and to pay the sum of $1000 therefor, represented to counter-claimant that the horse was sound in wind and limb, and free from any defect whatsoever.

2. That counterclaimant, believing defendant's statements to be true, and induced thereby, bought the horse paying the counter-defendant the sum of $1000 by the execution of a promissory note dated July 1, 1976.

Form 11: Counterclaim (continued)

3. That counter-defendant made the aforesaid representations knowing them to be false and with the intent to induce counterclaimant to make the purchase and to defraud him.

4. That the horse was in fact unsound, being then, and for a long time prior to the sale, inflicted with an incurable disease called cyphalothrixrhusiopathia.

5. That counterclaimant has expended the sum of $3000 in feeding and taking care of the horse and in endeavoring to cure him of the disease, and has been put to other expenses, embarrassment and humiliation.

Wherefore counterclaimant demands judgment against the counter-defendant for the sum of $3000 plus interest, court costs, expenses, attorney's fees, and for such other and further relief as to the court seems just and proper.

(Certificate of Service) (Signature)

Form 12: Cross-Claim

IN THE DISTRICT COURT

IN AND FOR ANYWHERE COUNTY

STATE OF ANYWHERE

Civil Action Number ____

Black Jack, Plaintiff, v. John Good, Defendant	)))))))	CROSS-CLAIM

Defendant, cross-claimant, sues the co-defendant ______________, and alleges:

1. (similar allegations as complaint or counter-claim).

(Certificate of Service) (Signature)

E. Third Party Complaint

Okay, you're not finished yet. In most courts a defendant may sue some other person not a party to the action who is or may be liable to him for all or part of the plaintiff's claim against him. Thus a controversy that otherwise would require more than one action for final determination can be resolved in one proceeding. The procedure is designed to save time and expenses and to avoid differing results from the same set of facts.

If a counterclaim is brought against the plaintiff, he may also bring in a third party. So, after you assert your defenses and claims against the plaintiff, you should assert your claims against anybody else in the whole world that may be liable or responsible in any way. The more you get in (in good faith) the less likely you will get shafted.

In some state courts the counterclaim, cross-claim, and third party complaint may not be recognized as such, but provisions are usually made for you to bring a separate action (called a cross complaint) against the plaintiff, a co-defendant or some third person not yet a party to the action. In these situations the judge will generally consolidate the cases which reaches the same results as the modern rules -- just one big happy family of litigants!

Form 13: Third Party Complaint

IN THE DISTRICT COURT

IN AND FOR ANYWHERE COUNTY

STATE OF ANYWHERE

Civil Action Number ____

Black Jack, Plaintiff,	)	
v.	)	THIRD PARTY COMPLAINT
John Good, Defendant	)	

Defendant, Third Party Plaintiff, sues ____________, Third Party Defendant, and alleges:

1. Plaintiff Black Jack, has filed against defendant a complaint, copy of which is attached hereto as Exhibit C.

2. (Here state the grounds upon which you are entitled to recover from third party defendant, all or part of what the plaintiff may recover from you. The allegations should be framed similar to those in the complaint and the counterclaim.)

Wherefore, Third Party Plaintiff demands judgment against the Third Party Defendant for all sums that may be adjudged against defendant in favor of plaintiff.

(Must be served on the third party with summons) (Signature)

Form 14: Motion To Bring In Third Party Defendant

IN THE DISTRICT COURT

IN AND FOR ANYWHERE COUNTY

STATE OF ANYWHERE

Civil Action Number ____

Black Jack, Plaintiff, v. John Good, Defendant	)))))))	MOTION TO BRING IN THIRD PARTY DEFENDANT

Defendant moves for leave to make ________________ a party to this action and that there be served upon him summons the third party complaint as set forth in Exhibit D, attached hereto.

(Certificate of Service) (Signature)

F. Discovery

Now, here's where the real fun starts. We come to the difference between the allegata and the probata (latin for allegations and proof). All you need for making allegations is a piece of paper and a typewriter. When the troops gather down at the courthouse the guy with the "evidence," "facts," "proof," will carry the day. Proper use of discovery proceedings is the easy--long--way to get it. If you use these techniques properly, you can find out every witness the other parties will call at the trial, all the testimony they have, all documents and records the other parties have and just about anything else you want to know about them. Anything that is relevant, or that may lead to the discovery of relevant evidence can be inquired into. You can have them and their lawyers beat to a frazzle before they recover from your Rule 12 motions.

A discovery program has three practical purposes:

1. to narrow the issues to those matters actually disputed;

2. to secure information regarding the existence of evidence that may or may not be used at trial;

3. to obtain evidence for use at trial.

The rules are designed to ensure against surprise, trickery, bluff and legal gymnastics at trial and to assist in achieving just results based on truth.

Informal discovery involves informal investigations, interviews, research, study and physical inspection outside the realm of formal discovery procedures under court rules. You can have a good time being a detective -- being your own investigator.

Under the discovery rules you can generally get any matter not priviledged, evidence relevant to the subject of suti, facts calculated to lead to the discovery of admissible evidence, some work product of the lawyers, and some opinions of experts.

The court discovery rules are so liberal now that practically anything is discoverable. In fact the federal rules were recently expanded to make them even more liberal. Most state court rules have not yet adopted these new changes, therefore we will use a sample of the state rules on discovery -- rather than the Federal Rules.

There are five major tools under the rules for discovery:

1. Depositions
2. Written interrogatories to witnesses
3. Written interrogatories to parties
4. Motion to produce documents, etc.
5. Request for admissions.

Rule 30: Depositions

This rule permits any party (you) to take the testimony -- under oath -- of any person, including a party, by deposition upon oral examination. You can do this anytime after you are served with summons and complaint as long as you give the party and witnesses reasonable notice under the rules. It is a simple procedure -- but relatively expensive as compared with the other tools you have available for use. You merely file in the court file -- with a copy to all parties -- a "Notice of Taking Deposition" stating the time and place and name and addresses of each person to be examined. You can also -- under most state court rules -- require the plaintiff to bring with him and produce designated documents, records, or other evidence you may want to look at, copy or ask the witnesses questions about. If you depose a witness who is not a party to the action, you have to arrange for him to voluntarily appear for the deposition or subpoena him. You don't have to subpoena a party. You must arrange for a court reporter (or other stenographer authorized to take depositions in your state) to transcribe the testimony and arrange to pay the court reporter a "sitting" fee plus the cost of typing up the testimony (if you decide to type it up -- usually not required). The fee may be $25 to $50 per day and the transcript may run from $2 to $3 per page depending on where you are, and who you get. In some states you may also use videotapes instead of a court reporter. This is a good plan if you have the equipment available.

You put the plaintiff (or witness) under oath and proceed to ask him just about any questions you want that are relevant to the suit (or your counterclaim). Read your court rules on this topic very carefully to make sure you follow all the requirements. This is more complicated -- and more expensive -- than the written interrogatories to a party, discussed later. But, if you have a few hundred dollars you can put the plaintiff through a ringer -- as many times as the judge will let you.

Procedural Tip: Here's a maneuver I have seen pulled a million times by a lawyer or party who wants to raise hell with an adverse party -- but not run up a bunch of fees for a court reporter. I've done it a few times myself! Notice the adverse party for his deposition in <u>your</u> office. Instead of hiring a court reporter get your secretary to "transcribe" the testimony. It doesn't matter if your secretary can't transcribe 5 words per minute -- just have her sit there with a pad and pencil and scratch like hell on her pad. Any person who is a notary can put the witness under oath -- or you may be able to do it yourself -- or let your secretary do it if no one challenges it. Ask all the questions you want -- relevant and irrelevant -- as many and as long as you like.

If the other party doesn't raise the question of the competency of the "court reporter" it may be waived -- at least you got your information without the cost of a reporter. If he raises it in advance you may have to "postpone" the deposition to a later date. You can do the same thing with other "witnesses" if you like. Don't be timid. You can't be too forceful in the defense of yourself.

Rule 31: Depositions Upon Written Questions

This procedure is similar to Rule 30, except that it is less expensive -- takes far more time -- and usually produces less evidence and is a lot less fun. But, if you are short on funds for discovery -- and don't have the stomach for pulling the old "deposition without a court reporter" procedural tip, supra , -- study this rule carefully and give it your best shot. But look at Rules 33, 34, and 36 first! We're only just beginning.

Rule 33. Interrogatories to Parties.

(a) Availability; Procedures for Use. Any party may serve upon another party written interrogatories to be answered by the party served or, if the party served is a public or private corporation, or a partnership, or association, or governmental agency, by any officer or agent, who shall furnish such information as is available to the party. Interrogatories may, without leave of court, be served upon the plaintiff after commencement of the action and upon any other party with or after service of the summons upon that party.

Each interrogatory shall be answered separately and fully in writing under oath, unless it is objected to, in which event the reasons for objection shall be stated in lieu of an answer. The answers are to be signed by the person making them, and the objections signed by the attorney making them. The party upon whom the interrogatories have been served shall serve a copy of the answers, and objections if any, within 30 days after the service of the interrogatories, except that a defendant may serve answers or objections within 45 days after service of the summons upon that defendant. The court may allow a shorter or longer time. The party submitting the interrogatories may move for an order under Rule 37(a) with respect to any objection to or other failure to answer an interrogatory.

(b) Scope; Use at Trial. Interrogatories may relate to any matters which can be inquired into under Rule 26(b), and the answers may be used to the extent permitted by the rules of evidence.

An interrogatory otherwise proper is not necessarily objectionable merely because an answer to the interrogatory involves an opinion or contention that relates to fact or the application of law to fact, but the court may order that such an interrogatory need not be answered until after designated discovery has been completed or until a pre-trial conference or other later time.

(c) Option to Produce Business Records. Where the answer to an interrogatory may be derived or ascertained from the business records of the party upon whom the interrogatory has been served, or from an examination, audit, or inspection of such business records, or from a compilation, abstract, or summary based thereon, and the burden of deriving or ascertaining the answer is substantially the same for the party serving the interrogatory as for the party served, it is a sufficient answer to such interrogatory to specify the records from which the answer may be derived or ascertained and to afford to the party serving the interrogatory reasonable opportunity to examine, audit, or inspect such records and to make copies, compilations, abstracts, or summaries.

This procedure is best for getting:

1. simple facts concerning background or foundational information, such as exact dates, witnesses, times and places;

2. admissions as to contentions that narrow or reduce issues;

3. exact names and addresses of persons and exact identification of relevant documents -- for further discovery;

4. specific facts supporting general allegations in pleadings or clarifying approximations in depositions; and

5. identification of trial experts and the substance of their opinions.

If the plaintiff doesn't answer or is vague, evasive -- ambiguous -- you can raise holy hell with a battery of motions, hearings and sanctions. Moreover, these little "procedural techniques" don't cost you any money and it takes a lot of time to finish it all. Give it a try, you'll like it.

> Rule 34. Production of Documents and Things and Entry Upon Land for Inspection and Other Purposes.
>
> (a) Scope. Any party may serve on any other party a request: (1) To produce and permit the party making the request, or someone acting on his behalf, to inspect and copy, any designated documents (including writings, drawings, graphs, charts, photographs, phono-records, and other data compilations from which information can be obtained, translated, if necessary, by the respondent through detection

devices into reasonably usable form), or to inspect and copy, test, or sample any tangible things which constitute or contain matters within the scope of Rule 26(b) and which are in the possession, custody, or control of the party upon whom the request is served; or (2) to permit entry upon designated land or other property in the possession or control of the party upon whom the request is served for the purpose of inspection and measuring, surveying, photographing, testing, or sampling the property or any designated objection or operation thereon, within the scope of Rule 26(b).

(b) Procedure. The request may, without leave of court, be served upon the plaintiff after commencement of the action and upon any other party with or after service of the summons upon that party. The request shall set forth the items to be inspected either by individual item or by category, and describe each item and category with reasonable particularity. The request shall specify a reasonable time, place, and manner of making the inspection and performing the related acts.

The party upon whom the request is served shall serve a written response within 30 days after the service of the request, except that a defendant may serve a response within 45 days after service of the summons upon that defendant. The court may allow a shorter or longer time. The response shall state, with respect to each item or category, that inspection and related activities will be permitted as requested, unless the request is objected to, in which event the reasons for objection shall be stated. If objection is made to part of an item or category, the part shall be specified. The party submitting the request may move for an order under Rule 37(a) with respect to any objection to or other failure to respond to the request or any part thereof, or any failure to permit inspection as requested.

(c) Persons Not Parties. This rule does not preclude an independent action against a person not a party for production of documents and things and permission to enter upon land.

Rule 36. Requests for Admission.

(a) Request for Admission. A party may serve upon any other party a written request for the admission, for purposes of the pending action only, of the truth of any matters within the scope of Rule 26(b) set forth in the request that relate to statements or opinions of fact or of the application of law to fact, including the genuineness of any documents described in the request. Copies of documents shall be served with the request unless they have been or are otherwise furnished or made available for inspection and copying. The request may, without leave of court, be served upon the plaintiff after commencement of the action and upon any other party with or after service of the summons upon that party.

Each matter of which an admission is requested shall be separately set forth. The matter is admitted unless, within 30 days after service of the request, or within such shorter or longer time as the court may allow, the party to whom the request is directed serves upon the party requesting the admission a written answer or objection addressed to the matter, signed by the party or by his attorney, but, unless the court shortens the time, a defendant shall not be required to serve answers or objections before the expiration of 45 days after service of the summons upon him. If objection is made, the reasons therefor shall be stated. The answer shall specifically deny the matter or set forth in detail the reasons why the answering party cannot truthfully admit or deny the matter. A denial shall fairly meet the substance of the requested admission, and when good faith requires that a party qualify his answer or deny only a part of the matter of which an admission is requested, he shall specify so much of it as is true and qualify or deny the remainder. An answering party may not give lack of information or knowledge as a reason for failure to admit or deny unless he states that he has made reasonable inquiry and that the information known or readily obtainable by him is insufficient to enable him to admit or deny. A party who considers that a matter of which an admission has been requested presents a genuine issue for trial may not, on that ground alone, object to the request; he may, subject to the provisions of Rule 37(c), deny the matter or set forth reasons why he cannot admit or deny it.

The party who has requested the admissions may move to determine the sufficiency of the answer or objections. Unless the court determines that an objection is justified, it shall order that an answer be served. If the court determines that an answer does not comply with the requirements of this Rule, it may order either that the matter is admitted or that an amended answer be served. The court may, in lieu of these orders, determine that final disposition of the request be made at a pre-trial conference or at a designated time prior to trial. The provisions of Rule 37(a)(4) apply to the award of expenses incurred in relation to the motion.

(b) Effect of Admission. Any matter admitted under this Rule is conclusively established unless the court on motion permits withdrawal or amendment of the admission. Subject to the provisions of Rule 16 governing amendment of a pretrial order, the court may permit withdrawal or amendment when the presentation of the merits of the action will be sub-served thereby and the party who obtained the admission fails to satisfy the court that withdrawal or amendment will prejudice him in maintaining his action or defense on the merits. Any admission made by a party under this Rule is for the purpose of the pending action only and is not an admission by him for any other purpose nor may it be used against him in any other proceeding.

The request for admission rule is the area where your personal knowledge of all the facts in your case can give you some real upmanship. On each of the good points in your case and each of the weak points in the plaintiff's case, hammer away at request for admissions of facts. If you don't get the right responses -- what you want -- pepper him with additional written interrogatories and make him explain his lies. If you don't get what you want file a series of motions and seek orders from the judge requiring plaintiff to answer "in accordance with the spirit of the rules." Of course, this may take some time. But who's in a hurry? And if you press plaintiff to making statements under oath that you can prove conclusively are false -- take it to the DA and put him in jail!

Each time you prove a "fact" which plaintiff refused to admit on your request for admission of facts you file a motion under Rule 37 to collect your costs, expenses and attorney fees. Now, this may take some time too. If his answers to written interrogatories are evasive or incomplete -- just file your motions. Be tough!

Rule 37(c) is as follows:

> (c) Expenses on Failure to Admit. If a party fails to admit the genuineness of any documents or the truth of any matters as requested under Rule 36, and if the party requesting the admissions thereafter proves the genuineness of the document or the truth of the matter, he may apply to the court for an order requiring the other party to pay him the reasonable expenses incurred in making that proof, including reasonable attorney's fees. The court shall make the order unless it finds that: (1) The request was held objectionable pursuant to Rule 36(a); or (2) the admission sought was of no substantial importance; or (3) the party failing to admit had reasonable ground to believe that he might prevail on the matter; or (4) there was other good reason for the failure to admit.

This is really a very important tool in your discovery work. You may not collect a lot of "attorney's fees" but you sure can wear the plaintiff and his lawyer to a nub.

If the plaintiff fails to answer written interrogatories or respond to any rule you may haul him down to the judge and get an order directing him to comply -- and in some cases you may get a court order providing:

1. That the matters regarding which the order was made or any other designated facts shall be taken to be established for the purposes of the action in accordance with the claim of the party obtaining the order;

2. An order refusing to allow the disobedient party to support or oppose designated claims or defenses, or prohibiting him from introducing designated matters in evidence;

3. An order striking out pleadings or parts thereof, or staying further proceedings until the order is obeyed, or dismissing the action or proceeding or any part thereof, or rendering a judgment by default against the disobedient party;

4. In lieu of any of the foregoing orders or in addition thereto, an order treating as a contempt of court the failure to obey any orders except an order to submit to a physical or mental examination.

In lieu of any of the foregoing orders or in addition thereto, the court shall require the party failing to obey the order, or the attorney advising him or both, to pay the reasonable expenses, including attorney's fees, caused by the failure, unless the court finds that the failure was substantially justified or that other circumstances make an award of expenses unjust. You can have a lot of fun with this rule if you follow all the procedures.

Suggested Discovery Strategy:

Now that you have reviewed the discovery rules, here's a few suggestions about how you can proceed to (1) whip saw a plaintiff to the point where he will wish he had never thought of suing you, (2) discover enough evidence and defenses to win the case one way or another -- either on procedural grounds or at trial, or (3) collect enough facts, records, documents, data, exhibits and other evidence to make a lengthy trial very distasteful to plaintiff and his attorney. In some courts -- in some cases -- justice doesn't always go to the kind at heart! You have to defend yourself -- nobody else will!

As soon as you get the summons and complaint go to the closest library and spend a day or two. Look up all the general law -- and statutory law of your state on the legal issue involved in your case. Contracts, bills and notes, debts, open accounts, guaranty, consumer contracts, breach of contract, loans, interest, usury, warranty, etc.

But -- do not ask him for legal advice: he will be embarrassed, he is not allowed to give it -- you may be embarrassed -- and that's not where you want to get your legal information. Go to the library for that. Listen to all he has to say about court procedures. Specifically ask the clerk what procedures are followed for getting a hearing on motions -- get a copy of local court rules that tell you all about this -- and be sure you understand the "hearing" procedures.

You should be able to get all this done in a few days after you get the summons and complaint.

Here's Your Plan: (for a typically "No Holds Barred" Case)

First: From your study of the complaint, your research of the law and your review of the affirmative defenses in the court rules, write down -- in draft form -- your answer to the complaint. Analyze the facts you have available and list two--three--four--of your best points. Offense and Defense. Concentrate on these points throughout the litigation. List all other possible points in your case -- offense and defense -- as a secondary battlefield.

Second: List in writing the two--three--four--weakest points in the plaintiff's case. Don't worry too much at this point about the evidence -- that comes later -- much later -- just list all the points in plaintiff's case a typical juror might be pissed off about. Put them down in writing with your answer and the Points And Defenses in Your Case.

Third: Roll out the Big Guns!

a. Propound your first set of written interrogatories to plaintiff (maybe 30 to 100) directed mainly to names and addresses of witnesses, identification "sufficient for identification and description in a motion to produce: of documents, records, exhibits and other "relevant" things in the case. There are several sets of books in the law libraries that give examples of the kind of questions for written interrogatories that pull the best answers.

b. File your first set of Request For Admission of Facts in which you request the plaintiff to admit all the good, factual points in your case. Especially the ones you know you can prove. Don't list controverted, vague, uncertain points -- or points you know he will deny -- use only those crisp, specific facts you know an honest (?) plaintiff would have to admit under oath. You may throw in one or two vague ones so you can later go to court on a hearing to compel a more direct answer. This may delay the case --but you can get a lot of information this way.

Keep in mind that this first set of written interrogatories is directed mainly at identifying where facts, information and evidence is located and who has it -- you'll get to that later. Don't rush!

c. Along with the Request For Admission of Facts consider (optional) filing a second set of written interrogatories in which you track your Requests on the major points in your case and the major weaknesses of plaintiff's case -- and on each point propound the following interrogatory: "If you deny Request For Admission 3, 4, etc., filed simultaneously herewith, explain specifically, with particularity, and in detail each and every fact, piece of evidence and reason why you made such denial under oath." Do this <u>only</u> for the big ones -- your good points you know you can prove if you have to.

Okay, this is your first salve! You now have a good analysis of your lawsuit and you have prepared a good outline of your trial. Let's go to work!

Fourth: How about some "Rule 12 Motions?"

Study rule 12 (or your comparable court rule) carefully and look at the annotations of the court cases that construe the rules. You must be familiar with the local cases construing your rules. A few hours in the law library (look in your state statutes for the general court rules applicable to the court you are in) will give you a good idea of how to handle the motions. Write down the citations to some of the cases -- and when time permits -- read them.

Here's your next move:

a. Consider a Motion To Dismiss (or demurrer) based on each of the points listed in Rule 12 (or comparable rule). Those that hold water -- use them -- file your motions, and be careful to file an affidavit -- or other evidence -- where needed to support your points.

b. Consider a Motion For More Definite Statement (or Bill of Particulars) on any points in the complaint that are vague or ambiguous.

c. Consider a Motion To Strike any "redundant, immaterial, impertinent, or scandalous matter" in the complaint. Use this motion carefully -- and cautiously. Read the local cases before using it.

d. Big Point: Repeat: Be Sure To Check Your Local Court Rules to determine whether a brief of memorandum of authorities is required when you file your motions. In some courts (especially the busy, over-crowded ones) the local rules provide that in some motions the parties have to file briefs, and the judge may rule on the motions without a hearing. If you fail to file a brief -- where required -- (usually filed with the motion -- or within 10 days) the judge usually denies your motion without looking at it -- and without giving you a fleeting thought. But look at it from the judge's point of view: he is busy -- sometimes over-worked -- and some lawyers file tons of paper -- for delay -- running up fees -- habit --

harrassment -- getting brownie points -- and some are perfectly proper procedures to prepare a case for trial (like yours). The judge requires the briefs to discourage the filing of so many motions.

You don't have to write a legal treatise -- the judge knows a hellava lot more about the rules and cases than you or most lawyers, but your job is to help him by writing down on paper the authorities he already knows about. It is a convenience for the judge, and typically it need be no more than a page or two. Sometimes only a citation to Rule 8, or to one or two cases on your specific point will do it. Besides, as indicated above, the judge knows the rules!

Fifth: File your counterclaims, cross-claims, and third party complaints where the facts justify it. Do not file any sham or frivolous pleadings, but if you have a good cause of action -- or probably have one -- go it at full speed. Don't hesitate to be a detective and investigator yourself to get facts and evidence. You can talk to the plaintiff's lawyer -- but not the party who has an attorney. You can talk to anybody else who is a potential witness -- hostile or friendly. Don't hesitate to "shake" them down for information and evidence -- this is only good preparation for the trial of your case. If a witness is reluctant to talk to you, you must explain in detail to him the rule of court on depositions -- and ask him if he wants that treatment -- an official subpoena -- official hearing -- under oath -- before an official court reporter who takes down every word he says. And don't just make empty threats -- be prepared to carry through with it if necessary.

The third party practice can be a little tricky, so study the rule carefully -- and try to file it before you file your answer -- so you don't (in most courts) have to get special permission from the judge.

Remember, don't file your answer until all the Rule 12 motions have been ruled on by the judge. Sometimes one of these motions can get lost in the shuffle of papers and as long as the judge hasn't ruled on it you don't have to file an answer. For example, I have seen a party file three Rule 12 motions -- arrange for a hearing on two of them -- write briefs -- and argue like hell -- and not schedule the third one for hearing. Frequently the plaintiff's lawyer will overlook it -- or forget it. So, after 6 to 12 months of hassling over your two motions you still don't have to answer unless the other party schedules a hearing on your third -- lost -- motion or the judge does it himself -- which is not likely.

Sixth: After you get plaintiff's answers to the first set of written interrogatories, sit down and carefully propound a second set of interrogatories (this may take a lot of questions) in which you ask specific, particular, exact questions about all the documents, records, evidence and witnesses the plaintiff told you about in his answers to your first set of written interrogatories. If plaintiff doesn't answer the interrogatories (first set or second set or any of them) to your satisfaction you simply file a set of motions and tell the judge about it! File another set of Request For Admissions of Facts, if appropriate.

Seventh: If plaintiff made objections to any of your written interrogatories of Request For Admissions of Facts just let them set there -- forever if possible. Don't you call his objections up for hearing yet. Even though some rules require a party to set his own objections for hearing, the lawyers are frequently too busy to do it, or he overlooks it. If the plaintiff ever proceeds further in the case you move for a continuance or call up for hearing his objections to your written interrogatories and file a Motion To Compel Plaintiff to Answer the Written Interrogatories. You see, this is all in accordance with the rules. Generally the plaintiff can't get his case set for trial until the pleadings are settled, and motions are disposed of. Don't hurry. They are not settled as long as motions are pending and undisposed of.

Eighth: After all the Rule 12 motions have been ruled upon by the judge -- file your answer. Set up all defenses available to you which you can support by evidence and get

(continued on page 3-72)

Form 15: Notice To Take Deposition

IN THE DISTRICT COURT

IN AND FOR ANYWHERE COUNTY

STATE OF ANYWHERE

Civil Action Number ____

Black Jack, Plaintiff,	))	
	)	NOTICE TO
v.	)	
	)	TAKE DEPOSITION
John Good, Defendant	))	

Notice is hereby given that defendant will take the deposition of plaintiff, Black Jack, at 9 A.M. on Tuesday July 19, 1977, at the offices of John Good, 123 First Street, City, State, before ________________, court reporter, or some other person authorized to take depositions in this state, said deposition to continue from day to day until completed.

(Certificate of Service)   (Signature)

Form 16: Written Interrogatories

IN THE DISTRICT COURT

IN AND FOR ANYWHERE COUNTY

STATE OF ARIZONA

Civil Action Number ____

Black Jack, Plaintiff,	)	
	)	WRITTEN INTERROGATORIES
v.	)	
	)	TO PLAINTIFF
John Good, Defendant	)	

Plaintiff is required to answer the following interrogatories in accordance with the applicable court rules:

1. (Here ask any and all questions that are relevant). See Bender's Forms of Discovery.

(Certificate of Service) (Signature)

Form 17: Request For Admissions

IN THE DISTRICT COURT

IN AND FOR ANYWHERE COUNTY

STATE OF ANYWHERE

Civil Action Number ____

Black Jack, Plaintiff,	)))	REQUEST FOR
v.	))	ADMISSIONS
John Good, Defendant	))	

Defendant, John Good, requests that plaintiff, within ____ days after service of this request, make the following admissions for the purpose of this action only and subject to all pertinent objections to admissability which may be interposed at trial:

1. That the documents described as Exhibits ___ herein are genuine.

2. That each of the following statements is true:

   a.

   b.

   c.

3. That the allegations contained in paragraph 3 of defendant's answer herein are true and correct.

Form 17: Request For Admissions (continued)

4. (Here list any other facts or issues). See Bender's Forms of Discovery.

(Certificate of Service) (Signature)

Form 18: Motion For Order Requiring Plaintiff To Answer Written Interrogatories

IN THE DISTRICT COURT

IN AND FOR ANYWHERE COUNTY

STATE OF ANYWHERE

Civil Action Number ____

Black Jack, Plaintiff, v. John Good, Defendant	)))))))	MOTION FOR ORDER REQUIRING PLAINTIFF TO ANSWER WRITTEN INTERROGATORIES

Defendant moves for the entry of an order directing the plaintiff to answer written interrogatories number 1, 5, 7, 8, 9, and 12 propounded on June 2, 1977, in accordance with the rules of court.

(Certificate of Service) (Signature)

ready to prepare for trial.

Ninth: Proceed with further discovery. Don't let up.

Tenth: Wait a while and if plaintiff ever wants to talk about settlement you might want to think about it. But don't hurry.

G. Devices For Terminating Litigation Without Trial

1. Voluntary Dismissal by Plaintiff

This happens more often than you think -- especially when a plaintiff pays his lawyer $1000 or more in fees on a $500 case he hasn't got to trial yet! It takes a while to wake him up. If you hammer away at discovery enough many lawsuits are forgotten. And paying a lawyer "for nothing" will get the plaintiff's attention.

2. Involuntary Dismissal

This may happen where a plaintiff fails to obey an order of court -- like an order to answer written interrogatories. The court simply dismisses his case if he does not comply with an order, or if he fails to comply with statutory requirements or court rules. If you press enough on discovery and motions you can't miss!

3. Lack of Prosecution

You can win many cases this way. Most courts have a rule that if the plaintiff takes no steps to prosecute his case (usually for one year) by bringing the case to trial it may be dismissed. Where you wear the plaintiff and his lawyer out with pleadings and discovery for a few months they will frequently lose interest in pushing the case to trial. Just let it lie there. This is likely to happen where a plaintiff gets tired pouring money into the lawyer's bank account, but has too much pride to take a voluntary dismissal -- he won't mind letting the case die a natural death. And the lawyer won't care either. You'd be surprised to know the number of violent fights I've seen between plaintiffs and their own lawyers. You can generate this kind of situation if you keep the pressure on.

4. Motion For Judgment On The Pleadings

This Rule 12 motion is not much: it is similar to a motion to dismiss (demurrer) and is based on the proposition that the pleadings are insufficient as a matter of law to establish a claim or defense. You can try it anyway if you have good grounds.

5. Motion For Summary Judgment

Now, this is a Big One !!

Rule 56. Summary Judgment

(a) For Claimant. A party seeking to recover upon a claim, counterclaim, or cross-claim or to obtain a declaratory judgment may, at any time after the expiration of 20 days from the commencement of the action or after service of a motion for summary judgment by the adverse party, move with or without supporting affidavits for a summary judgment in his favor upon all or any part thereof.

(b) For Defending Party. A party against whom a claim, counterclaim, or cross-claim is asserted or a declaratory judgment is sought may, at any time, move with or without supporting affidavits for a summary judgment in his favor as to all or any part thereof.

(c) Motion and Proceedings Thereon. The motion shall be served at least 10 days before the time fixed for the hearing. The adverse party prior to the day of hearing may serve opposing affidavits. The judgment sought shall be rendered forthwith if the pleadings, depositions, answers to interrogatories, and admissions on file, together with the affidavits, if any, show that there is no genuine issue as to any material fact and that the moving party is entitled to a judgment as a matter of law. A summary judgment, interlocutory in character, may be rendered on the issue of liability alone although there is a genuine issue as to the amount of damages.

(d) Case Not Fully Adjudicated on Motion. If on motion under this rule judgment is not rendered upon the whole case or for all the relief asked and a trial is necessary, the court at the hearing of the motion, by examining the pleadings and the evidence before it and by interrogating counsel, shall if practicable ascertain what material facts are actually and in good faith controverted. It shall thereupon make an order specifying the facts that appear without substantial controversy, including the extent to which the amount of damages or other relief is not in controversy, and directing such further proceedings in the action as are just. Upon the trial of the action the facts so specified shall be deemed established, and the trial shall be conducted accordingly.

(e) Form of Affidavits; Further Testimony; Defense Required. Supporting and opposing affidavits shall be made on personal knowledge, shall set forth such facts as would be admissible in evidence, and shall show affirmatively that the affiant is competent to testify to the matters stated therein. Sworn or certified copies of all papers or parts thereof referred to in an affidavit shall be attached thereto or served therewith. The court may permit affidavits to be supplemented or opposed by depositions, answers to interrogatories, or further affidavits. When a motion for summary judgment is made and

> supported as provided in this rule, an adverse party may not rest upon the mere allegations or denials of his pleading, but his response, by affidavits or as otherwise provided in this rule, must set forth specific facts showing that there is a genuine issue for trial. If he does not so respond, summary judgment, if appropriate, shall be entered against him.
>
> (f) When Affidavits Are Unavailable. Should it appear from the affidavits of a party opposing the motion that he cannot for reasons stated present by affidavit facts essential to justify his opposition, the court may refuse the application for judgment or may order a continuance to permit affidavits to be obtained or depositions to be taken or discovery to be had or may make such other order as is just.
>
> (g) Affidavits Made in Bad Faith. Should it appear to the satisfaction of the court at any time that any of the affidavits presented pursuant to this rule are presented in bad faith or solely for the purpose of delay, the court shall forthwith order the party employing them to pay to the other party the amount of the reasonable expenses which the filing of the affidavits caused him to incur, including reasonable attorney's fees, and any offending party or attorney may be adjudged guilty of contempt.

Summary judgment is the procedure by which cases coming within its scope may be disposed of quickly, without delay and without the necessity of trial when the facts show that there is in fact nothing to be tried.

The purpose of the summary judgment rule is to avoid the time, labor and expense to counsel, parties, court and jury involved in an unnecessary trial. If it appears at the hearing of a motion for summary judgment that there actually is no substantial controversy as to any material fact and that the movant is entitled to a judgment as a matter of law, the advantages of early recognition of that situation are obvious.

This motion is my favorite. It attacks the "merits" of the plaintiff's case, and is designed to pierce the pleadings to show that plaintiff's case has no merits based on the evidence, regardless of what is alleged in the complaint. The old difference between the allegata and the probata.

The basis for the motion is that looking at all the evidence, we see no genuine issue as to any material fact, and that you are entitled to a judgment as a matter of law. This is usually filed after discovery proceedings and is normally based upon admissions made in pleadings, depositions, testimony, answers to written interrogatories, answers to request for admission of facts, or matters of which judicial notice may be taken by the court.

But one of the most common sources of evidence -- the easiest and most frequently used for this purpose -- is an affidavit. Your affidavit must be based on personal knowledge (not hearsay), and must show that the person giving the affidavit or statement is competent to testify as to the matters stated in the affidavit. Usually you can file this motion at any time -- even with your answer in the proper case.

Generally, if the affidavits or other evidence filed with the court raise no genuine triable issue of fact, then the court must enter summary judgment for the moving party. Indeed, there would be nothing to do at trial. You ought to read the annotations under this rule to get a good idea of the kind of cases the judges will give summary judgment on. Here is an example:

Suppose you got sued by John Doe for $50,000 on a $30,000 gambling debt (illegal in your state) and a $20,000 loan he made you 12 years ago (assume a 10-year statute of limitation in your state). You could file your answer under oath admitting the gambling debt, and admitting the "loan," but allege that gambling is illegal in your state and that the 10 year statute of limitations had run on the "loan." You file a Motion For Summary Judgment. You Win! No trial. Same result with most of the affirmative defenses.

Hot Tip: In some cases where you have a good, clean defense you can state all the evidence, facts and circumstances of your defense in your answer -- verify it -- sign it under oath -- and file it. In a few days file a simple short form motion for summary judgment without any supporting affidavits or other evidence (remember you put it all in your answer and swore to it under oath). Later routinely call it up for hearing. Frequently lawyers -- busy ones -- young, inexperienced ones -- sloppy, lazy ones -- will overlook the verified answer and simply appear at the hearing -- or send a young associate -- to argue the motion. If the facts and evidence in your answer show there is no genuine issue -- and plaintiff does not controvert your facts -- you are entitled to a summary judgment as a matter of law.

Second Tip: Note that Rule 56(d) (and most state court rules) provides that the court at the hearing of the motion, by examining the pleadings and the evidence before it and by interrogating counsel, shall, if practicable, ascertain what material facts exist without substantial controversy and what material facts are actually and in good faith controverted. It shall thereupon make an order specifying the facts that appear without substantial controversy, including the extent to which the amount of damages or other relief is not in controversy, and directing such further proceedings in the action as are just.

This procedure is almost like a pre-trial conference, but you can sneak up on a lot of lawyers -- the overworked, inexperienced, lazy, sloppy ones and gain many advantages with this maneuver. It works great with the verified answer ploy. See Long Form Motion For Summary Judgment, page 3-80. You can sneak up on some lawyers easier than another lawyer -- they won't be expecting this kind of move from a layman.

Form 19: Motion For Summary Judgment (Short Form)

IN THE DISTRICT COURT

IN AND FOR ANYWHERE COUNTY

STATE OF ANYWHERE

Civil Action Number ____

Black Jack, Plaintiff, v. John Good, Defendant	)))))))	MOTION FOR SUMMARY JUDGMENT

Defendant moves for the entry of a summary judgment in favor of the defendant and against the plaintiff on the grounds that there are no genuine issues of any material facts and defendant is entitled to a judgment as a matter of law. This motion is based upon the pleadings, affidavits, depositions and answers to written interrogatories filed in this cause (including affidavit attached hereto as Exhibit E.)

(Certificate of Service) (Signature)

Form 20: Motion For Summary Judgment (Long Form)

IN THE DISTRICT COURT

IN AND FOR ANYWHERE COUNTY

STATE OF ANYWHERE

Civil Action Number ____

Black Jack, Plaintiff,	)	
	)	MOTION FOR
v.	)	
	)	SUMMARY JUDGMENT
John Good, Defendant	)	

Defendant moves for the entry of a summary judgment in favor of the defendant and against the plaintiff on the grounds that there are no genuine issues of any material fact and that defendant is entitled to a judgment as a matter of law. In the alternative, if judgment is not rendered upon the whole case or for all the relief asked and a trial is necessary, the Court at the hearing of the motion, by examining the pleadings and evidence before it and by interrogating counsel and the parties, ascertain what material facts exist without substantial controversy and what material facts are actually and in good faith controverted, and make an order specifying the facts that appear without substantial controversy, and directing such further proceedings in the action as may be just and proper.

Form 20: Motion For Summary Judgment (Long Form) (continued)

(Note: This kind of motion is generally not appropriate in personal injury cases or in cases which turn primarily on adjudication of fact questions, but is more generally applicable to situations in which there are or may be several questions of law raised by the complaint and several issues of law raised by defenses which should be determined by the trial court prior to trial.)

(Certificate of Service) (Signature)

Form 21: Final Summary Judgment

IN THE DISTRICT COURT

IN AND FOR ANYWHERE COUNTY

STATE OF ANYWHERE

Civil Action Number ____

Black Jack, Plaintiff,	)	
v.	)	FINAL SUMMARY JUDGMENT
John Good, Defendant	)	

This cause came on for hearing on Defendant's motion for summary judgment and the court having reviewed the file, heard arguments of counsel and the parties, and being fully advised in the premises finds that there are no genuine issues of material fact and that defendant is entitled to a judgment as a matter of law, and it is therefore

ADJUDGED that the motion is hereby granted and judgment is hereby entered in favor of the defendant and against the plaintiff and the defendant shall have his costs upon appropriate application for which let execution issue.

Done and ordered this ___ day of June, 1977, at City, State.

____
Judge

H. Pre-Trial Conference

Rule 16. Pre-Trial Procedure; Formulating Issues.

In any action, the court may in its discretion direct the attorneys for the parties to appear before it for a conference to consider

(1) The simplification of the issues;

(2) The necessity or desirability of amendments to the pleadings;

(3) The possibility of obtaining admissions of fact and of documents which will avoid unnecessary proof;

(4) The limitation of the number of expert witnesses;

(5) The advisability of a preliminary reference of issues to a master for findings to be used as evidence when the trial is to be by jury;

(6) Such other matters as may aid in the disposition of the action.

The court shall make an order which recites the action taken at the conference, the amendments allowed to the pleadings, and the agreements made by the parties as to any of the matters considered, and which limits the issues for trial to those not disposed of by admissions or agreements of counsel; and such order when entered controls the subsequent course of the action, unless modified at the trial to prevent manifest injustice. The court in its discretion may establish by rule a pre-trial calendar on which actions may be placed for consideration as above provided and may either confine the calendar to jury actions or to non-jury actions or extend it to all actions.

Some courts require a pre-trial conference, some make it discretionary with the judge; some do neither. Check your local rules and customs. Generally this is influenced by the attitude of the local judges and this is one of the "local" rules, practices and customs you need to ask the clerk about. Most judges use the rule to some extent.

Where the pre-trial conference is held, it is usually informal, usually in the judge's chambers, and only attorneys or parties attend. No witnesses or evidence is presented. Most judges first explore the settlement possibilities and then follow their own version of the schedule in Rule 16. Some judges prepare the pre-trial order -- most do not; some ask one of the lawyers to prepare the order. If the judge asks the other lawyer to prepare an order make sure you ask the judge to let you help -- don't trust the lawyer on the other side. He will give you the shaft every chance he gets -- and he will usually be sanctimonious about it. Sometimes you can convince the judge at the pre-trial conference that you are entitled to a summary judgment, and he has the power to grant it at the pre-trial conference even if you have not filed a formal motion for summary judgment.

Form 22: Motion For Continuance

IN THE DISTRICT COURT

IN AND FOR ANYWHERE COUNTY

STATE OF ANYWHERE

Civil Action Number ____

Black Jack, Plaintiff, v. John Good, Defendant	)))))))	MOTION FOR CONTINUANCE

Defendant moves for a continuance of the trial in this action on the following grounds:

1. The cause for continuance arose after setting of the action for trial and is due to circumstances beyond defendant's control.

2. This action is one for ____________. In order for defendant to establish his defense, it will be necessary to prove ___________ (set forth issues in case).

3. The only person having knowledge of these facts is _________________ who is now at ___________________. He will testify as follows: ___________________ (set forth the testimony).

4. Defendant has exercised due diligence to obtain the presence of the witness at trial. The following steps

Form 22: Motion For Continuance (continued)

have been taken (list them).

5. Despite defendant's acts, the witness will not be available because (give reasons), but defendant believes the witness will be available on _____________ because _________________ (set forth facts showing reasonable grounds to believe witness will be present at that time).

6. The procedure for taking of the witness' deposition in this case is not satisfactory because (give reason).

(Certificate of Service)   (Signature)

Form 23: Order Granting Motion For Continuance

IN THE DISTRICT COURT

IN AND FOR ANYWHERE COUNTY

STATE OF ANYWHERE

Civil Action Number ____

Black Jack, Plaintiff, v. John Good, Defendant	)))))))	ORDER GRANTING MOTION FOR CONTINUANCE

This cause was heard on defendant's motion for continuance of the trial and it is:

ADJUDGED as follows:

1. The Motion For Continuance is granted.

2. The action previously scheduled for trial on _____________ is reset for trial on ____________.

Done and ordered this ___ day of _________ at City, State.

____
Judge

CHAPTER IV

TRIAL

Here's where you can really have a blast!

A trial is defined as the judicial investigation and determination of issues between the parties to an action. State statutes and court rules provide for the manner and procedures by which cases are placed on the trial calendar and outline the general order in which cases on the trial calendar will be disposed of. A great deal is left to the discretion of the trial judges.

The U. S. Constitution, Seventh Amendment, says, "In suits at common law, where the value in controversy shall exceed twenty dollars, the right of trial by the jury shall be preserved." Most states also have a similar constitutional provision.

Caveat: Your right to a jury trial is dependent upon timely demand. In federal courts you must make a demand in writing and file it in court within 10 days after the filing of the last pleading (usually your answer) directed at any issue upon which the jury trial is sought. In the state courts there is usually a similar requirement; check your court rules.

In preparing for the trial you will need to do research on court procedures, watch some trials -- as many as you can -- and have your complete outline of everything you will present to the jury at trial. Write it all down -- don't rely on your memory. And make sure you get all of your points, facts and evidence in the record. Your evidence is not good unless the jury hears it and (on appeal) unless the court reporter gets it down in writing. And make sure you get all your defenses supported by evidence, where you have it. While this will be the most fun part of handling your own case, you will have to do some serious work and research in preparing your evidence and learning the basic proceedings in a jury trial even though the judge may give you help from time to time. Still, this is much better -- far more fun -- far more rewarding and productive -- and far less expensive than paying a lawyer to do something you can do yourself.

A. Invoking the Rule

Before your trial starts you may (in most states) invoke the rule. This means that any party may ask the judge to order all witnesses in the case (except the parties) to stay out of the courtroom during the trial (and not talk to other witnesses) so they do not hear other witnesses testify. The purpose of excluding witnesses from the courtroom is to prevent them from listening to testimony of the other witnesses and then shaping or fabricating testimony accordingly. Generally this is a good idea -- unless you want your witnesses to hear the others testify. If you wish to invoke the rule make sure you do it <u>before</u> the trial begins.

B. Objections to Evidence; Motion To Strike Evidence; Motions For Mistrials

A party has the right to have his objections ruled on, and if that right is not recognized by the trial judge, with the result that improper evidence is introduced to his prejudice, there is reversible error. Even if a judge asks a witness an improper question the party should object and insist on a ruling by the court.

In order to preserve the right to have a question reversed on appeal, a party must make his objection known at the earliest appropriate opportunity in order to give the trial judge the opportunity to take appropriate preventive or corrective action. In other words, you don't reverse a trial judge on appeal unless you give him a chance to rule the right way at the trial.

When objections are made reasons or grounds for the objections must be given. The old objection that the questions are irrelevant, immaterial and incompetent is the all time favorite, but you don't usually get too far with it. You have to be specific on your grounds.

A motion to strike out evidence is the appropriate procedure where a witness is permitted to answer after objection to the question propounded to him, or where the witness, in response to a question which is relevant and proper, gives an incompetent answer. A motion to strike is proper where there has not been an opportunity to object previously because the question did not indicate the nature of the answer.

A motion for mistrial should be made where prejudicial evidence is introduced, or where opposing counsel makes improper or prejudicial statements in the presence of the jury. As a defendant you should scream for a mistrial at every opportunity. Plaintiff may not be so anxious for a retrial after he pays his lawyer's fees.

C. Selection of Jury

The easiest way to learn all about this proceeding is to watch two or three or more jury trials in the court -- talk to lawyers -- court bailiffs -- court watchers -- court reporters -- judges -- and others who are familiar with court proceedings. You need to know the local practice on jury challenges -- the number of jurors -- their qualifications -- what to ask on void dire (qualification of jurors). Then go to the library and check the statutes -- rules -- and cases -- and the Official Jury Instructions for your court.

D. Opening Statement by Plaintiff

You can count on many lawyers to tell the jury about plaintiff's case -- then proceed to tell the jury what a dirty bastard you are. Don't get in the gutter with him -- take the high road -- of dignity --truth--honor. But if he gets out of bounds -- object and move for a mistrial. Interrupt opposing counsel in his opening and make a motion for mistrial only if you know you have good grounds -- or that you can gracefully gain some good points with the judge and jury. Opening statements are properly for outlining to the jury the evidence to be presented -- not for argument of your case.

E. Opening Statement by Defendant (You)

Be dignified -- respectful -- friendly (but not oversolicitous) to the judge and jury. Don't say bad things -- directly -- about anybody. In your opening statement to the jury (1) outline the good points of your case in terms of facts and evidence (not arguments) that you plan to present to them, and (2) describe for the jury the facts and evidence about the plaintiff's case -- but only the weak points -- not his strong points -- ignore his good points at this time. Remember you are an advocate -- not an objective observer -- and you owe it to yourself to put forth your side of the case. Essentially you want to tell the jury about your case and in the process they will learn a great deal about you.

F. Presentation of Evidence by Plaintiff

1. Direct testimony by plaintiff: Watch for "leading" questions and hearsay. Make your objections when you know you are right. Don't give the judge a "pain in the neck" by making frivolous objections.

2. Your cross examination of witnesses and careful examination of every exhibit:

If you think one of plaintiff's witnesses is lying you can attack his credibility. Make sure you have support for your position. You can ask him: "Have you ever been convicted of perjury?" "Do you have some special reason for not telling the truth in this case?" Take your time to examine any exhibit the plaintiff offers in evidence. Remember, you don't have to cross examine every witness. Cross only if you can help your case.

G. Motion For Directed Verdict

Unless you are relying entirely on your affirmative defenses to win your case you should always make a motion for a directed verdict at the close of plaintiff's case. Check your rules and statutes and have all the "grounds" available for this motion and be sure you state them to the judge. You must state your grounds and reasons; have them written down in your outline.

H. Presentation of Your Evidence

1. Direct testimony: Be sure you write down the questions before trial -- and know what the answers will be from all your witnesses -- and all opposing witnesses. Don't give the plaintiff an opportunity to repeat his best points -- your chances of pulling a Perry Mason are zero. When a plaintiff lies once he will lie the second time much easier! And he usually sticks to it 'til hell freezes over.

2. Plaintiff's cross examination of your witnesses: Don't let him badger -- intimidate -- or villify your witnesses. Make objections to the judge only. Don't argue or wrangle with the attorney for plaintiff -- always make your remarks to the judge or jury. Talking to the opposing lawyer in open court is almost always bad -- it's a loser -- you can't convince him of anything and you only give him help. You work with the judge -- stay on his side -- and work with the jury.

I. Plaintiff's Presentation of Rebuttal Evidence

Generally plaintiff can put in evidence and facts about the evidence you brought out in your case -- only to rebut your evidence.

J. Presentation of Your Rebuttal Evidence

In some courts, in some cases, you can have another chance to put in evidence -- but only to rebut plaintiff's new rebuttal evidence.

K. Motion For Directed Verdict

After all the evidence is in and both parties rest their case make your Motion For Directed Verdict again! State your grounds again in the record. Have your grounds carefully written down on paper so you can read the appropriate ones to the judge at the proper time -- don't rely on your memory.

L. Opening Argument by Plaintiff to Jury

Some attorneys make snide remarks about the adverse party -- or their case -- and while there is a wide direction in what can be said you should object to any personal attack, or matter that is clearly improper.

M. Your Argument to Jury

Plaintiff gets the open and close to the jury, so this is your only shot -- make the most of it. You should develop the idea throughout the trial that you are the "good guy" and the plaintiff and his attorney are vicious scoundrels. In your argument show the jury how you proved the points in your case that you told them about in the opening statement -- show them how the plaintiff's case was weak -- on the points you mentioned -- and how you and the jury will work the whole thing out to make a final determination that will result in truth and justice. Avoid appeals to sympathy, passion and prejudice, the golden rule argument, race, religion, political, social, class or business prejudices; pointing out wealth or poverty of litigant, appeal to self-interest of jurors as taxpayers, use of abusive language, or attack on the other party or his attorney. Stick with facts -- evidence -- and the law. The "golden rule" argument is telling the jury to place themselves in the place of one of the parties. They are supposed to be objective in their deliberations.

N. Closing Argument by Plaintiff

You can count on plaintiff to give the jury his best shot here so you must plan your argument well to convince the jury to rule in your favor -- no matter what the "shyster" says or does by way of trying to pull the wool over their eyes.

O. Judge Gives Jury Instructions

Make sure you give the judge your proposed instructions at the proper time -- and object to plaintiff's proposed instructions that are not correct statements of the law.

P. Jury Verdict, Entry of Verdict and Entry of Judgment

After the verdict no matter who wins somebody has to prepare a written judgment for the judge to sign and "enter" in the court records to make it final. Each court has its own practice but it is usually prepared by (1) the clerk, (2) the attorney of the party who wins, (3) the judge (not likely), (4) the judge's secretary, or (5) a combination of the above. If you win be sure it is entered and you get a copy of it. If you don't win, be sure the other side doesn't put something in the judgment that is improper -- watch those lawyers!

Burden of Proof: The plaintiff has the ultimate burden of persuasion as to the essential elements of his claims. You -- the defendant -- have the ultimate burden of persuasion on your affirmative defenses raised in the pleadings. Every court has a standard instruction on this point and will always give it to the jury.

Preponderance of Evidence: The burden of persuasion is to produce whatever evidence is required to convince the trier of fact (jury). In civil cases the judge will always instruct the jury that this proof must be by a "preponderance" of the evidence, as opposed to "beyond every reasonable doubt" as required in criminal cases.

"Preponderance" of evidence is usually defined as a situation where one side of the case is made to appear more likely or probable to the trier of fact. It is evidence that when weighed with that opposed to it, has more convincing force, so that the probability of truth lies therein. It is that evidence which is most convincing and satisfying in the controversy between the parties, regardless of which party may have produced such evidence.

Trial Technique Tip: As a defendant you can develop a mighty powerful argument to the jury about the might burden of proof the law <u>imposes</u> on the plaintiff. Use terms like "Plaintiff must prove all essential elements of his lawsuit by a Preponderance of the evidence (emphasize <u>Preponderance</u> -- as though it were the weight of the world) -- by a "Preponderating weight of all the <u>credible</u> evidence" (emphasize <u>credible</u> -- and later tell them plaintiff's evidence simply is not credible). Each argument you make on the good points of your case should end with the observation that "<u>and the burden of proof is on the plaintiff</u> to prove his case by a preponderance of the evidence." That's a quick switch -- from your good points to plaintiff's burden -- but true. Just don't bother to dwell on who has the burden to prove your defenses. In a close case this argument can make the difference. Keep in mind that most jurors don't know a lot about court procedures -- you have a right and duty -- as your own counsel -- to tell them. And make them know it!

Second Tip: In your final summation to the jury consider a wind-up something like this:

"And Ladies and Gentlemen of the Jury......"

(1) Explain in high sounding phrases the high honor--duty--obligations-- the jury has in maintaining truth and justice (lay this one on heavy -- but sincere);

(2) Repeat the old "preponderance of the evidence" theme as to the entire case of plaintiff and every part of it;

(3) Summarize the good points of your case -- and the weak points of plaintiff's case; and

(4) End with a flag waving "we who labor here seek only the truth." Put your own personal touch and personality to it and let your imagination and emotions flow.

Jury Instructions: Before the case is submitted to the jury for a verdict, the trial judge will give the jury instructions to guide their deliberations. Typically, the instructions will specify the issues in dispute; which party has the burden of proof (persuasion) on each issue; the rules of substantive law applicable to each issue; the kinds of verdict the jury may return; the procedure to be followed in deliberation and reaching a verdict. Federal courts, and many state courts, permit the trial judge to comment on the evidence to the jury. Most judges do not.

The ultimate responsibility for instructing the jury rests with the trial judge, and failure to provide correct and complete instructions on every material issue in a case is judicial error. But, in a practical sense, counsel -- or the party -- owes a duty to the judge to call to his attention any error in the instructions which he proposes to give, to enable him to review and correct the instructions before the matter is submitted to the jury.

Generally, the trial judge must instruct the jury on whatever theories of the case are reasonable supported by the evidence, regardless of whether he personally believes that evidence. Each party has an absolute right to have the jury instructed in accordance with his version of the facts in the record. Make sure you get the judge to cover all your points.

Practically all the state courts have an official approved set of "Jury Instructions," usually approved by the state Supreme Courts. You can find this in most law libraries -- and some public libraries and it is very important for you to have this to get your proper instructions to propose to the trial judge. Actually, these instruction books are easy to use, but you have to be careful not to overlook any theory of your case. It is your responsibility and not necessarily the judge's to find the law.

Closing Arguments: In most civil trial courts the argument to the jury comes before the judge gives the instructions, rather than your brilliant argument. Therefore, you must make a dynamic impression on the jury so they will remember the important points in the jury room. If you have good facts -- the thrust of your argument should be on the facts -- if you don't have good facts argue the law; if you don't have either - smile.

If your facts and evidence are not especially great on your side of the case talk about honesty, integrity, charity, truth, justice, credibility of witnesses, fairness, honor, fidelity, right, equity, trustworthiness, freedom from fraud and chicanery, sincerity, candor, innocence, plain-talk, clean hands, fair play, self-respect, square dealing, loyalty to principles, impartiality of the jury......and that sort of thing.

And associate yourself and the jury with all of these good qualities and with truth and justice.

Don't sling mud. Don't call plaintiff dirty names. Don't be rude to plaintiff's lawyer, the judge, jury or anybody else. You are Mr. Clean! Ignore the real damaging evidence of plaintiff, if any.

Preparation For Jury Summation: Always have a written outline of your summation to the jury and be sure to cover all the points. Practice your "winding-up" part to make sure you can deliver it with conviction--emotions--and fire!

Hot Tip: One of the ploys I always enjoyed -- in some cases -- where there was one major issue of law that controls in the case, was to explain -- very seriously -- that the judge will give the jury the law that controls the case. But, tell them, your case is founded on one main issue. Explain that while it is the judge's statement of the law that counts you just want them to know that you are relying on one main issue of law in your case. Then read verbatim from what you know the judge is going to tell them about your legal issue. Yell and scream to the jury that this is the "KEY" issue in the case -- what the case is really all about. When the judge tells them your theory of the case -- just as you told them -- they will gain a new respect for you and your knowledge of the law. And maybe they will agree with you.

Role of the Trial Judge: The trial judge may, in his discretion, either question any witness called by a party, or even call and question witnesses of his own, but most judges usually exercise this power sparingly, in order to avoid claims of partisanship or prejudicing the jury. And a few states even deny the right to trial judges to call or ask questions of witnesses -- on the ground that the trial judge must act as an "umpire", not as an advocate. Even so, when you represent yourself, if you conduct yourself with dignity and a knowledge of your case and your rights, the trial judge will usually be very helpful in giving you some assistance in following the correct court procedures.

Form 24: Final Judgment

IN THE DISTRICT COURT

IN AND FOR ANYWHERE COUNTY

STATE OF ANYWHERE

Civil Action Number ____

Black Jack, Plaintiff, v. John Good, Defendant	)))))))	FINAL JUDGMENT

This cause came on for jury trial on the 28th day of August, 1977, and the jury having returned a verdict in favor of the defendant it is

ADJUDGED as follows:

1. Final Judgment is hereby entered in favor of the defendant, John Good, and against the plaintiff, Black Jack, and the defendant shall go hence without delay.

2. Defendant shall be entitled to costs on appropriate application for which let execution issue.

Done and ordered this ___ day of __________ at City, State.

____
Judge

CHAPTER V

POST TRIAL MOTIONS AND MANEUVERS

You're not down yet. If the jury goes wrong -- as some of them do -- or if the judge makes a mistake by making some reversible error -- you can handle it. There are several remedies you can employ to attack the trial court before resorting to an appeal.

A. Motion For Judgment Notwithstanding the Verdict (non obstento veridicto)

A judgment N.O.V. nullifies the jury verdict; it is a judicial determination that regardless of the verdict, the evidence is legally insufficient to sustain the verdict and therefore you are entitled to a judgment in your favor. This is the same position you took when you filed your first pleading -- don't ever back down from your position if you are right.

Generally the motion can be filed only (1) in jury trials, (2) if you made a motion for directed verdict at the close of plaintiff's case and/or at the close of all the evidence, and (3) if you make your motion timely (usually within 10 to 15 days after the verdict -- or, in some courts, the entry of judgment).

B. Motion For New Trial

This is generally filed at the same time you file your motion for judgment N.O.V. Typical of the grounds on which a new trial may be granted in actions at law are:

1. Irregularities in proceedings, for example, counsel's comment in argument on the poverty of plaintiff and the wealth of defendant, false answer by juror on voir dire examination, etc.;

2. Misconduct of jury in deliberations or verdict;

3. Accident or surprise, for example, some extraordinary event that was prejudicial to you -- against which you exercised due diligence in seeking to protect yourself, and where you sought relief (like a motion for mistrial, request for continuance, etc.) at the earliest possible opportunity;

4. Insufficiency of the evidence (ride this one all the way);

5. Newly discovered evidence that you -- through due diligence -- could not have obtained before trial;

6. Verdict or decision is against the law;

7. Excessive or inadequate damages.

C. Motion To Vacate or Amend Judgment

This motion is directed to your steadfast efforts to have the judge change the judgment to correct errors of law -- especially your argument that the evidence is insufficient to sustain the verdict.

D. Motion For Relief From Judgment or Order

This motion is generally filed to correct clerical errors or mistakes, on grounds of inadvertance, surprise, excusable neglect of party or counsel, newly discovered evidence which by due diligence could not have been discovered in time to move for a new trial or fraud, misrepresentation or other misconduct by the other party, that the judgment is void as a matter of law, that it has been satisfied, or that a prior judgment upon which it is based has been reversed, or any other reason justifying relief from the operation of the judgment.

E. Independent Suit to Set Aside Judgment

The grounds for this kind of action are:

1. Jurisdictional defects (lack of subject matter jurisdiction or lack of personal jurisdiction); and

2. Extrinsic Fraud or Mistake.

F. Appeal

If you have come this far you can handle your own appeal, but we are counting on you to win your case in the trial court.

CHAPTER VI

SETTLEMENT DISCUSSIONS

A. Where Plaintiff Has An Attorney

There are generally three types of lawyers who represent plaintiffs:

1. Bad,
2. Bad; and
3. Very Bad.

But to be more realistic, there are, indeed, three categories of lawyers that you will have to learn to deal with. They are:

1. Settlers -- about 50 percent of them,
2. Sometimes trial lawyers if forced to it -- about 40 percent,
3. Trial Tigers -- about 10 percent.

The first category -- the settlers -- is a piece of cake. He would go to jail before he would try a case. You would be surprised to know how many there are. I have seen many lawyers who called themselves "trial" lawyers -- that didn't try _one_ case per year. If you get one of these you should make him know your plan to go to trial if necessary. Then forget it -- he'll never go to trial. If he can't settle, convince his client to drop it, let it die a natural death -- or some other "disposition" he may sometimes hire a real "trial" lawyer to handle the case for him.

The "sometimes settler" seldom goes to trial -- but he will on some cases. Your odds are very good that you can settle with these guys for 30 to 50 percent of the claim.

The "Trial Tiger" is a rare breed. There are very few of them, they don't usually handle "small" cases, and if you are unlucky enough to get one of these on the other side -- you're in trouble. He's not as interested in "justice" or fairness as he is in kicking your guts in. He loves combat and he prepares his cases -- and he wins. Maybe you can wear him down, but if you can't get some "disposition" of the case he will clean your wagon. Your chances are very good that most of your opponents will be "settlers."

Don't trust any of them! Don't ever call them first about settlement; let them bring it up. In most cases there will almost always come a time when plaintiff's attorney will want to discuss settlement. Most lawyers who represent collection agencies, lending institutions, or big companies don't make their money by going to trial. Plain fact is, they generally don't like to go to trial at all, and although they put up a big front many of them would resort to most anything to avoid a trial. Oh, I don't mean a conscious, deliberate sellout -- swindle -- or double-cross. I mean that many lawyers are so busy making money in "negotiating" settlements -- they really don't have time to bother with a trial. So, whether they are conscious of it or not you can "negotiate" them right down, down, down in their demands to where you want them, especially as you get close to the trial date. And if you force them to go to trial you generally won't have to worry about getting at least one or two continuances of the trial -- they will probably ask for it. If so, you can reluctantly agree to a continuance and tell them "anyway we can probably settle this case" -- but don't settle unless you get your terms.

When the subject of settlement first comes up -- do not make any offer. Try to be very friendly -- professional -- with the lawyer, ask him about certain aspects of plaintiff's case that you tell him you "don't quite understand," ask him about the judge, the court procedures, the law, his case -- everything. Try to get friendly -- buddy-buddy -- with him and he might tell you all you want to know about the case and other topics as well. You see, he may want to get friendly with you so he can take you to the cleaners with his own perfected "settlement strategy". Watch it! Not all lawyers will do this -- but some will. Try it.

Don't make any offer -- just keep asking him questions and keep asking him to come down on his "outrageous" demands in view of the "circumstances involved in this case." But don't tell him what you mean by "circumstances." Let him imagine.

Tell him his demands are too high, his client is not telling him the "whole story," but don't tell him what you mean and don't tell him about your case. Just ask him more questions -- friendly like. If he doesn't come down to your settlement figures as the trial date approaches you may consider sending him a check made out in his name "as attorney for plaintiff." Mark it "in full and complete settlement of case No. ____, entitled ___________ v. ___________, etc. Say in your covering letter, "...... here is the settlement we talked about." Don't explain anything. You can make it clear to the lawyer that if he doesn't take the check -- he's out -- maybe he'll get nothing.

Second Ploy: If you can't wrap it up with the attorney a few days before the trial tell him you know he is awfully busy, that his client really isn't so bad and that if he will give you his "permission and authority" to discuss it with the plaintiff personally you can probably settle the case -- and not have to "bother" him and his busy schedule. That you and he will probably have to postpone the trial -- it seems such a waste of time for the lawyer to go to trial -- especially where a settlement is so close, and he has far more important cases to handle! Once you start talking directly to the plaintiff personally you can usually just forget about the trial. Plaintiff's lawyer may not bother to reschedule a trial date or would agree to another postponement if needed. Don't settle with plaintiff unless you get your terms, but always continue to keep the discussions alive. There may come that day you're looking for when plaintiff gets tired paying his lawyer "for doing nothing."

Meanwhile, be sure you are hammering away at them with pleadings, motions, discovery proceedings and preparing your own case for trial -- this keeps the meter running on the other side. Be ready if you have to go to trial. And make them know it! Your big hammer is the discovery process. Be tough. If you use it effectively very few plaintiffs will ever get to trial.

Your main objective in settlement discussions include:

1. delay,
2. put pressure on plaintiff and his lawyer,
3. get a low settlement,
4. get trial postponements
5. get facts and evidence about plaintiff's case,
6. learn all you can about plaintiff's case, court rules, laws, and anything else you can get from the lawyer, but check out the law yourself -- don't trust him,

7. generally raise a lot of hell just for the hell of it.

B. Where the Plaintiff Has No Lawyer

If plaintiff does not have a lawyer, you can drive that "turkey" crazy. Always hold out hope to him that you will be able to work out a "satisfactory" settlement with him. "Satisfactory" settlement means on your terms. Don't make him so mad he won't talk. Use your arguments -- suggestions of bankruptcy -- expenses of litigation -- and your continued hopes of settlement in between pelting the hell out of him with motions and discovery proceedings. With the use of the procedures and strategies outlined in this book you will seldom have to pay any money at all.

CHAPTER VII

SMALL CLAIMS COURTS

A. Development of the Small Claims Courts in this Country

The development of small claims courts in the United States is the result of reformist activity at the beginning of this century. The reformers, among them some of the most outstanding legal scholars of their day, were particularly interested in relieving the legal and monetary difficulties experienced by the less affluent litigants and the individuals with a valid but small monetary claim. In some states these people could turn to the justice of the peace courts, but these tribunals were confined to certain areas and were notorious for the low quality of justice they provided. Thus, no legal institution existed to deal adequately with small claims at that time.

One of the early advocates of the small claims courts was Dean Roscoe Pound who said:

> It is here that the administration of justice touches immediately the greatest number of people. It is here that the great mass of an urban population, whose experience of the law in the past has been too often experience only of the arbitrary discretion of police officers, might be made to feel

> that the law is a living force for securing their individual as well as their collective interests. For there is a strong social interest in the moral and social life of the individual. If the will of the individual is subjected arbitrarily to the will of others because the means of protection are too cumbrous and expensive to be available for one of his means against an agressive opponent who has the means or the inclination to resist, there is an injury to society at large.
>
> Pound, The Administration of Justice in the Modern City, 26 Harvard Law Review 302 (1913).

The general purpose of small claims courts is to provide a summary procedure for the litigation of small claims; that is, claims not exceeding a certain specified amount -- usually $500 to $1000. Therefore, certain legal technicalities that may encumber an ordinary proceeding are generally dispensed with in a small claims proceeding. However, the substantive law applicable in a small claims proceeding is the same as that applicable in a regular proceeding.

Typical of the court rules in small claims courts is that of New York which provides:

> The court shall conduct hearings upon small claims in such manner as to do substantial justice between the parties according to the rules of substantive law and shall not be bound by statutory provisions or rules of practice, procedure, pleading or evidence.
>
> New York Civil Court Act Article 18, Section 1804 (McKinney Supp. 1972).

This is, of course, a perfectly reasonable provision, as cases involving very complicated substantive rules or important questions of law can and should be removed by the judge to the regular civil courts.

The formal rules of evidence should not apply to small claims procedures. The report of the National Institute for Consumer Justice states that a court attempting to force adherence by all small claims litigants to the rules of evidence would have no time to devote to the substance of the cases before it. Because of the relative informality of most consumer transactions, the majority of the consumers do not receive or retain the evidence necessary to conform to the formal rules of evidence. A Philadelphia small claims court rule -- in response to this reality -- provides:

> When a claim is based upon a written contract, three copies of at least pertinent portions must be filed with the statement of claim. However, if the contract is not available, it is sufficient simply to explain why and describe its provisions.
>
> Philadelphia Municipal Court Civil Procedure Rule 107(e) (1971).

B. Small Claims Court Rules

The proceedings in Small Claims Courts are designed and written to operate without lawyers. This is good. The court procedures and rules in trial courts of general jurisdiction tend to slow down, impede, and complicate litigation. Small claims courts are just the opposite; they are geared up for quick, swift, speedy, sudden -- final justice. Contrary to the prevailing view of most people about judges, virtually all of the Small Claims Court Judges are honest, diligent, hard-working, dedicated public servants of the people. They are genuinely and truly interested in helping society in one of its biggest problems -- settling local, small claims that frequently are charged with deep emotions and explosive anger.

But, this is not to say that you can't delay a case in small claims courts. It is a challenge, but with the right attitude, a good plan, and a lot of brass you can wrap the plaintiff in tight little bundles of nerve and bounce him off the walls 'til he will think his head is in a clanging glockenspeil.

C. Asserting Your Defenses

Here's your plan:

One: Don't work on the judge -- or look to the Small Claims Court Rules to drag out, delay, or complicate the case. Most of the rules do not have discovery-Rule 12 motions or any of the stuff you (and lawyers) use in the main trial courts. In this court you have a totally different set of procedures to work with. But don't let that slow you down.

<u>Two</u>: Work on the Plaintiff.

Here's why: Look at the Small Claims Court Rules; study them carefully. Typically, there is no deposition rule, no Request For Admissions rule, no Written Interrogatory rule, and no Rule 12 motions rule! Can you believe it? On first glance you'd think this doesn't give you much room to maneuver. It's okay; the judge knows this, but in all probability the plaintiff doesn't. And even if he has a lawyer who knows it you can still accomplish your mission.

Most Small Claims Court Rules don't have the "goodies" we talked about in the other courts, however most do permit counterclaims. Most of them do have a reference to some circumstances under which the other court rules can be used. Most of these provisions require permission from the judge to use the regular Court Rules. Small Claims Court Judges are lawyers and most of them like to get interesting legal issues in their court. Generally most cases in the small claims courts fail to generate interesting -- and significant -- legal issues for the judge to decide. This is your golden opportunity. Give him some.

It is to your advantage to catch the judge's attention and present him with some not-so-dull legal questions.

<u>Three</u>: File a written answer. Review Chapter III and set up every possible defense available to you. Remember

if you have any doubt about the availability of evidence to support the various defenses mentioned in Chapter III you can always ask the plaintiff about it in your Written Interrogatories, Request For Admissions and Depositions. Don't worry if your Small Claims Court Rules don't have a requirement -- or specific procedure -- for filing an answer. Most of them do. But file it anyway. If there is any doubt about it file a separate motion seeking court authorization. Any time you are in doubt about procedures, file a motion asking the judge what to do. I have never known of a judge who would deny a request for filing defenses. If you have a good defense -- especially if it includes affirmative defenses -- and if the plaintiff -- or any other witness -- has evidence relating to your defense you can get it okayed by almost any court.

Your answer and motions should be filed right away -- don't wait until a few days or a week before the trial date. In fact, you ought to do it within a week or two after receiving the complaint -- well before the trial date.

As we discussed up front you may very well have a valid counterclaim against the plaintiff. File it. And if the amount of your counterclaim exceeds the jurisdictional amount of the court you will have grounds to ask to have the case transferred to a higher court - where you have a legal right to use all those "tactics." But take this warning: Do not file any unfounded counterclaim or fabricate or exaggerate the amount. Most rules have a severe penalty for this. Lawyers did this routinely when the small claims courts first started and the rules and judges come down hard on false claims like this. If you file "phony" claims to oust the Small Claims Court of jurisdiction the judge will put your head in a glockenspeil and give it a double clang!

Where you do not have a counterclaim sufficient to transfer the case to a higher court you may have other grounds to have it transferred. Most Small Claims Court Rules have a special provision on this point and you might as well give it a shot.

Four: Find some written authority in the rules -- or otherwise -- to file the kind of motions normally filed in courts of general jurisdiction. Some do, some don't. Generally there is a provision in the Small Claims Court Rules that provide for filing of pleadings like those authorized by the main court rules -- under certain circumstances. If you can't find satisfactory written authority somewhere -- in the rules--statutes--case laws--then you just naturally assume that all litigants have such rights and file them anyway. Sounds fair, doesn't it? You can cite constitutional due process--natural law--fundamental equitable principles--or the need to avoid a miscarriage of justice. Make your arguments sincere and give them with conviction and most judges will go along with it. If they do, you're okay. If they don't you can accomplish your objectives anyway. Don't budge an inch.

Five: Review Chapter III on the Rules of Court and map out a plan as though you are operating under those rules. File sets of written interrogatories and file a written motion asking the judge to give you permission to do it. File a Request For Admissions and a written motion asking the judge to give you permission to do it. File any other motion you can think of along with a motion requesting permission to do it. And don't forget to file a Notice To Take Deposition of the plaintiff--in your office --at your convenience.

D. Tactics and Techniques For Winners

Now, the idea is not to file a bunch of motions for the judge to rule on. You want to put the plaintiff on the defensive. After you hit him a few times he will start to get the drift of your thinking -- he's got a hellava fight on his hands. If human nature takes its natural course the plaintiff will make a call -- early in the game -- to talk about a settlement. Don't budge. Except on your terms.

If you can't flush him at this point -- on your terms -- file a motion for a continuance of the trial date. In all probability (certainly in most small claims courts) the case will automatically be set (by the clerk) for trial within 30 to 60 days after the filing of the action. And it is a general practice for the clerk to give one or two postponements of the trial date with only a telephone request; try it. This is the usual routine; you can count on it. Your motion for continuance of the trial date will be based on the grounds, among all the others you can think of, that there is pending before the court -- and undisposed of -- several motions directed toward various procedural issues, but primarily involving discovery. Surely a fair-minded judge would not require the trial of a case where one of the parties has not had a reasonable opportunity to properly defend himself! This is a good argument even though some Small Claims Court Rules expressly provide that "Depositions and discovery shall be unavailable in small claims procedures." You can't possibly defend yourself without getting the answers to your Written Interrogatories, Request For Admissions, and the other evidence the plaintiff has adamantly failed and refused to allow you to obtain. Sounds like a denial of constitutional due process of law to me!

To recap: You got sued in Small Claims Court. You (1) check the rules carefully, (2) file an answer asserting your denials and defenses, (3) file any counterclaims you may have against the plaintiff with a motion to transfer the case to a higher court (if appropriate), (4) file all the discovery procedures available under any court rules, (5) file a separate written motion in each instance -- asking the judge for authorization to utilize the pleadings and discovery procedures you have filed, (6) file a motion for continuance of the trial date because the pleadings and discovery have not been concluded. File a few written Briefs to support your legal points -- and to keep them awake.

There are a variety of things that generally happen at this point:

1. You can, in all probability, get one, two, three or more "stipulated" or "agreed" continuances of the trial date. The other side will usually be agreeable to postponements of the trial -- whether by attorney or pro se.

2. If the plaintiff is represented by an attorney you can be virtually assured -- with the ineluctability of a syllogism -- of one of two results: (a) continuous postponements of the trial or (b) plaintiff's legal fees will cause the case to die a natural death! It is easy for a clerk to "lose" a case that gets postponed a half dozen times.

Can't you just imagine how fast the plaintiff's legal fees will skyrocket? No lawyer in his right mind would proceed in a case against <u>you</u> without doing his "homework". Expensive! The more he does the further you are from trial -- home free.

3. Settlement discussions -- on your terms -- are high on the list of probabilities.

4. If some settlement does not occur and you have to go to a hearing or a trial you can be sure that if you do your research and make an adequate argument the judge will (1) grant your motion for continuance, and (2) grant some of your pending motions to aid you in discovery and proper preparation of your defenses.

In the unlikely event you ever get to a trial you should consider these moves:

Before any evidence or testimony is taken ask the judge -- with strong conviction and confidence -- what he did with your pending motions. Caveat: Make sure you understand what he tells you. Ask him to explain it again if you do not fully understand. Lawyers and judges talk in circles a lot. If he says they were--or are--denied simply make an oral motion to renew each and every motion you have filed. Make another motion for continuance (orally) giving all the grounds stated in your previously filed motion plus any others that may have arisen (unavailability of witnesses, for example). After you make these oral motions say:

"Your Honor, I wish to be heard on the legal issues raised by the pending motions, and specifically, I wish to make it clear -- for the record and for this court -- the exact nature of the constitutional rights I am asserting in this case." Once you get his attention -- you unload both barrels. Be prepared to argue each of your points and to appeal the case, if appropriate.

In the remote possibility you get this far without terminating the case on your terms you must be prepared to go forward with the trial. Review the previous discussions about preparation for trial, have your exhibits marked and all your records and other evidence ready to go. When all the evidence is in -- but before the judge makes a decision -- make an oral motion for the judge to reserve judgment in the case and keep the case "open" to authorize you to introduce additional evidence at a later date. This is like a partial continuance; you get a final shot. Argue to the judge that his failure to grant your motions relating to discovery denied your rights to due process of law and you want to put in more evidence. You can generally do this either by further testimony, affidavits, exhibits or records.

In all events you will have had an experience that is -- for most people -- educational, productive, rewarding, and exciting. And you are a winner. The right side will have prevailed. Which reminds me of the famous quote from Winston Churchill that:

> "The truth is incontrovertible;
> malice may attack it,
> ignorance may deride it -- but in the end,
> there it is!"

CHAPTER VIII

MISCELLANEOUS

A. How To Use Law Libraries and Your Public Libraries

You don't need any special legal training to do the legal research needed to handle your own case in accordance with the instructions in this book. You will need time, interest, and perseverance -- but that's necessary for success in anything. Once you get into it you will enjoy it.

As you know lawyers go to law school for three years to learn "all the laws about everything" and to learn how to research and find "all the laws on everything." You will have only the subject of your lawsuit to research; your research is concentrated only on those legal issues raised in your case -- a case you know more about than anybody else in the whole world. Your research is, therefore, much easier and shorter, and not "all over the ball park." Moreover, you will have a keen and genuine personal interest in the legal issues in your case which makes it easier. Under these conditions you will become an "expert" on the laws in your case in a very short time. It's easier than you think.

There are several places where you can get the information needed to handle your case. The following are listed in order of preference as to the number of books available.

1. Law School Libraries

This is the place where you can find just about everything available anywhere. There is one or more in every state and you won't have any difficulty locating one. Most are state-supported schools and the libraries are open to the general public. Caveat: Be sure you don't mark any books or damage them in any way, and make sure you always follow all library rules about the use of the books and library. Librarians and law students are great helpers in finding anything you want. Law students are especially anxious to demonstrate how much they know about legal research, and law book, and the law. Strike up conversations with them (when they have the time) and they can be very helpful. You should dress appropriately for the atmosphere in a law library, do not make noise or distract any other users of the library -- and other persons won't generally cause any trouble for you. Once you get charged up about your research, you'll really have a lot of fun.

Some large law school libraries (usually in a large metropolitan area) charge a small fee for use of the library. In this situation the law library is always packed full of lawyers, professors, students, and other users anyway, therefore you are probably better off to go to the public library. Most public libraries in large cities have all the books you need.

You may want to look at several sources of law, but essentially the following sources are all you really need:

a. Your state statutes and court rules;

b. Digest of your state court decisions;

c. Your court "Jury Instructions;" and

d. Case Reports for your state.

1. University Libraries (especially a Business Department branch or library)

Most of these libraries have a copy of your state statutes, some have the case reports, and some have the Jury Instructions. These are generally public libraries and you should have no difficulty in finding what you need. Check the index first, and the librarian second!

3. State Supreme Court Library

If you live close to your state capitol where your state Supreme Court is located, you're in luck. You can use these, but be sure you put on your best "dignity" and manners. Actually you don't find many supreme court judges there, but their law research clerks will be swarming all over the place. And here is where you may be in luck. If you can strike up a conversation with these guys you're really in tall cotton -- you've got it made. They generally know all the laws, all the current decisions, all the court rules, and all about all the trial judges. Don't ask them for legal advice, but ask them about general law issues -- the issues you have in your case, and ask where to find the law. They know. They will be the most helpful people you will ever find. In a tough legal problem you might hire them -- for a small fee -- to do some research for you. They will do a better job than most lawyers and charge less.

4. State Courthouse Law Libraries

This is the law library for the trial judges. Most are available for your use, and they almost always have everything the judges have available, therefore all you will need. Also, check to see if the trial judges have a law clerk. Some do; some don't. These research clerks are usually overworked, but they can also be very helpful in giving you tips about the trial judges, the court procedures, where to find the law you need, and just about anything else you need in a law library. Naturally, the law librarian in all libraries is one of the best persons to consult. There's nothing wrong with your talking to the judges -- just don't talk to the judge on your case <u>about the facts in your case.</u>

5. Public Libraries

Most general public libraries have the state statutes, and some have the Jury Instructions and the Case Reports. The librarians and research clerks in these libraries are generally most helpful.

6. Lawyer Office Libraries

Most lawyers have access to all the basic sources listed above. Get friendly with some lawyer in the bigger firms in your town (they generally have more books), possibly retain him for some simple legal task (maybe writing a will). Most will be very cooperative in letting you use their books if you take good care of them and cooperate with his secretary. In a large firm you will always find the youngest lawyers buried in the law library. They are always easy to talk to and they are also anxious to show off about how smart they are. Ask them a few questions and see how much free information you can get. In all events you can have a handy library if you play it right.

If your case is fairly complicated and involves a substantial amount of money -- go to one of the younger lawyers in a big law firm. Talk to him about him representing you in your case. Don't make any commitment -- talk to him about his fee arrangement -- what tactics he might take if he handles the case, etc. After he quotes you a fee arrangement tell him you simply can't afford a lawyer -- "at this time" -- but can you "use his library to look up the law in your case" with the idea that you <u>may</u> be able to retain him (at his price) before the trial. Don't make any definite commitment -- leave it loose. In most circumstances he will be most anxious to help you find the law, and he may visit with you about your case during coffee breaks from time to time! Who knows, you just may want to retain him to help you try the case. At least it's a darn good option to have available. Besides, you need a handy law library. Don't hesitate to ask.

Final word on libraries - and research: You can learn more from judges' research clerks, law students and other court personnel in a day than you can learn pouring over law books for weeks. But you should do both -- just be efficient about it -- take some short cuts. Ask questions of everybody in sight -- make notes -- and then go to the library to search out the law you were told about.

Generally you won't need to buy any books, except that you should consider buying (or getting) a copy of the Court Rules (about $5 to $15) and a copy of the local court rules (frequently no cost or a nominal charge).

B. Pre-trial Attachment of Property

The United States Supreme Court has rendered a series of decisions during the past few years holding that state statutes authorizing prejudgment seizure of personal property, without notice to the owner, and without affording him an opportunity to be heard prior to the seizure, violate procedural due process of law standards under the Federal Constitution, where the statute in question is not narrowly drawn to meet some extraordinary situation requiring special protection to some state or creditor interest. See Fuentes v. Shevin, 407 U.S. 67 (1972); Mitchell v. W. T. Grant Co., 416 U.S. 600 (1974); and North Georgia Finishing, Inc. v. Di-Chem, Inc., 419 U.S. 601 (1975).

This rule has been applied to various property rights including welfare benefits, parole revocation, probation revocation, revocation of driver's licenses, forfeiture of airman's certificate, forfeiture of child custody, termination of unemployment compensation benefits, tenure at state colleges, tenancy in public housing, social security payments, mechanics liens, self-help repossessions under the Uniform Commercial Code, and many others. In Hamrich v. Ashland Finance Co. of West Virginia, 423 F.S. 1033 U.S.D.C. S.D. W. VA (1976) it was held that the West Virginia detinue statutes were facially unconstitutional as violative of both the Fourth Amendment prohibition against unreasonable searches and seizures and the due process clause of the Fourteenth Amendment insofar as they provided for a court clerk or justice, upon the filing of a conclusory affidavit, with no discretion but to issue a writ compelling an officer of the state to break in and seize items and insofar as they authorize the officer executing the writ to break into any place where property may be found... See also First Recreation Corporation v. Amoroso, 558 P 2d 917 (Ariz 1976).

You should check these cases in the event any effort is made to seize your property.

C. Defaults

If you fail to respond to a summons and complaint within the time prescribed, the plaintiff is entitled to have a default entered against you. Your failure to plead is considered as an admission of the claim against you. The fact that you don't plead within the time doesn't always mean that a default is automatically entered. Generally, in most courts, the plaintiff or his attorney has to file some application with the clerk or judge requesting the "entry" of a default. In other words, unless the plaintiff takes some steps the file will just sit there. If you file your pleadings before plaintiff charges down to get his "entry" you are home free. Frequently a lazy, sloppy, busy, lawyer will let a file lie around for weeks without entering a default. Therefore, even if you don't make it on the last day always check the court file to see if the default has been entered. If not, file. Quick!

After the entry of a default, the plaintiff must then go further and have a default judgment entered against you. If plaintiff is suing on a promissory note or other contract for a sum certain (liquidated damages), the judgment may be entered directly by the clerk or the judge. In all other cases, plaintiff must present his evidence to the court to obtain the judgment. In some courts he must give you a notice of hearing on the damage issue to give you an opportunity to contest the amount of the claim.

After a default has been entered you may also make a motion with the court to set aside the default. There are time limits (frequently 1 year) within which to file and the usual grounds include:

(1) that you have a valid excuse for the default -- excusable neglect, fraud, inadvertance, etc; and

(2) that you have a good and meritorious defense to the action, and (generally) you must file your proposed answer showing your defenses.

Frankly, this is a hard way to go -- just be careful not to let them enter a default against you.

CHAPTER IX

LAWYERS, JUDGES, COURTS AND YOU

Who Is The Judge?

Lawyers and judges are human just like you and me.

But when people spend all that time going through college, law school (learning big words) and a few years of law practice,they tend to form the idea they are some kind of God.

When they get appointed or elected as a judge -- they are God!

Well, that story may not be all true, but it is one of the legends that many people believe to be true. Judges have a constitutional duty to uphold the constitution and laws of the land -- that is their full-time job. They are human, and while human beings have flaws most of the judges try hard to do the right thing. But what is right for you -- in your case -- is your job. Judges make mistakes; it is your job to correct them if they happen to make a mistake in your case -- by appeal. Don't be afraid of judges; and don't think you are imposing on them by taking their time to try your case -- that's their job.

Your Attitude

In any contest (especially lawsuits) being aggressive is one of the essential elements of success. And you have to look like, act like, have the attitude of, and be, a winner. The word "law" is defined as "rules of civil conduct," or as I like to say, "the rules of the game by which life is played." Certainly in a court of law -- where you are engaged in a lawsuit--a contest--you have to play according to the rules laid down in that forum (court). The judge is the referee who can be reversed by a higher court. The Supreme Court (of last resort)--right or wrong --has the final word in this part of the game--the law. But what happens in your case depends more on you and what you do in preparation than on the other side, the judge or the Supreme Court.

Preparation

Your attitude about lawyers, judges and court personnel will play a big part in your success -- or lack of it. But let me give you the key word to describe your key to success -- in lawsuits and in life: PREPARATION!

In law school all my professors kept saying, "preparation for trial is the key to success as a lawyer. Prepare." My reaction was, "Hell, I know that; everybody knows that." Perhaps that's your thoughts. But it didn't take me very long after starting law practice to <u>understand</u>

what was meant by preparation. It doesn't matter whether you are by nature an aggressive person, a quiet, easy-going person, a big- or little-ego person, or somewhere in between. If you prepare your case well, you are a winner. If your lawsuit is important to you -- and it is -- you will be motivated to work hard and get "psyched up" about it. Spend all that excess energy in digging, investigating, examining witnesses, finding facts, getting exhibits, gathering evidence, doing your research and all the items we have discussed about preparing your case for trial.

You and Your Case

Judges preside over hundreds of cases; lawyers handle many cases. To them your case is just another case on a docket sheet. But to you it is your case. That's important. And it's big. You know more about it than anybody else, you can learn all about the specific laws governing your case, and you can be in charge of your case as it passes through the courthouse on a long list of other cases. If you prepare it well, all will end well.

Winners and Losers

In our society what is right, wrong, ethical, moral, sinful, proper, illegal, dirty, unfair, lawful, or inequitable is frequently a matter of opinion and has many shades of grey. Ask Bert Lance. Or Richard Nixon. When you, in your honest opinion, are right you shouldn't let rain, sleet, snow or the dark of night deter you in your quest for justice.

TEAR 'EM UP, TIGER!

GLOSSARY

Accord and Satisfaction: An agreement between two persons, one of whom has a right of action against the other, that the latter should do or give, and the former accept, something in satisfaction of the right of action different from, and usually less than, what might be legally enforced.

Action: A suit or process at law; the procedure of instituting a lawsuit in a court of law.

Adhesion Contract: A contract printed as a standard form, submitted by one party to the other on a take-it-or-leave-it basis. Adhesion contracts are commonly presented to consumers in situations where the buyer's position is substantially weaker than the seller's.

Affidavit: A written or printed declaration or statement of facts made voluntarily, and confirmed by the oath or affirmation of the party making it, taken before an officer having authority to administer oaths.

Affirmative Defenses: New matter constituting a defense; new matter which, assuming the complaint to be true, constitutes a defense to it.

Allegations: The assertion, declaration, or statement of a party to an action, made in a pleading, setting out what he expects to prove.

Allegata et probata: Latin; Things alleged and proved. The allegations made by a party to a suit, and the proof adduced in their support.

Annotations: A remark, note, or commentary on some passage of a book, intended to illustrate its meaning. Citations of cases construing statutes or other laws.

Answer: Strictly speaking, it is a pleading by which defendant in suit at law endeavors to resist the plaintiff's demand by an allegation of facts, either denying allegations of plaintiff's complaint or confessing them and alleging new matter in avoidance, which defendant alleges should prevent recovery on facts alleged by plaintiff.

Arbitration: The submission for determination of disputed matter to private unofficial persons selected in manner provided by law or agreement.

Assumption of Risk: Exists where none of fault in injury rests with plaintiff, but where plaintiff assumes consequences of injury occurring through fault of defendant, third person, or fault of no one. It is based upon the maxim "volenti non fit injuria," which means that to which a person assents is not regarded in law as an injury.

Attachment, See Writ of,

Averment: A positive statement of facts, in opposition to argument or inference.

Bankruptcy: The state or condition of one who is a bankrupt; amenability to the bankrupt laws; the condition of one who has committed an act of bankruptcy, and is liable to be proceeded against by his creditors therefor, or of one whose circumstances are such that he is entitled, on his voluntary application, to take the benefit of the bankruptcy laws. The term is used in a looser sense as synonymous with "insolvency," -- inability to pay one's debts; the stopping and breaking up of business because the trader is broken down, insolvent, ruined.

Bailiff: One to whom some authority, care, guardianship, or jurisdiction is delivered, committed, or intrusted. Court official.

Best Evidence: Primary or original evidence. The best and highest evidence of which the nature of the case is susceptible, not the highest or strongest evidence which the nature of the thing to be proved admits of. A written instrument is itself always regarded as the primary or best possible evidence of its existence and contents; a copy, or the recollection of a witness, would be secondary evidence.

Bill of Particulars: Written documentation of particulars in connection with and relevant to a law suit, specifying items, dates, times, and so on, submitted either voluntarily or on court order. An account of the items of a claim.

Bona fide: In good faith.

Breach of Contract: Failure, without legal excuse, to perform any promise which forms the whole or part of a contract.

Breach of Warranty: A violation of an agreement as to condition, content, or quality of a good sale, not involving fraudulent misrepresentation.

Brief: A written or printed document, prepared by counsel to serve as the basis for an argument upon a cause in an appellate court, and usually filed for the information of the court.

Burden of Proof: The necessity or duty of affirmatively proving a fact or facts in dispute on an issue raised between the parties in a cause.

Cause of Action: The fact or facts which establish or give rise to a right of action, the existence of which affords a party a right to judicial relief. See discussion in Chapter III.

Certificate of Service: A statement or assertion that a pleading document in litigation has been served upon the opposing party in the litigation.

Citation: 1. The reading, or production of, or reference to, legal authorities and precedents, (such as constitutions, statutes, reported cases, and elementary treatises), in arguments to courts, or in legal textbooks, to establish or fortify the propositions advanced. 2. A writ issued out of a court of competent jurisdiction, commanding a person therein named to appear on a day named and do something therein mentioned, or show cause why he should not.

Civil Action: An action wherein an issue is presented for trial formed by averments of complaint and denials in answer to new matter.

Civil Court: Courts vested with jurisdiction to handle civil controversies as distinguished from criminal cases. Many courts do both -- have concurrent jurisdiction.

Clerk: A person employed in a public office, or as an officer of court, whose duty is to keep records or accounts.

Co-defendant: A joint defendant.

Commence: To perform the first act of. To institute. To demand something by the institution of process in a court of justice.

Common Law: The general and ordinary law of a community receiving its binding force from universal reception. Historically, that body of law and juristic theory which was originated, developed, and formulated in England.

Complaint: The first pleading on the part of the plaintiff in a civil action. Its purpose is to give defendant information of all material facts on which plaintiff relies to support his demand.

Compulsory Counterclaim: Claim by defendant against the plaintiff arising out of the same transaction or occurrence as stated in the complaint.

Consideration: The inducement to a contract. The cause, motive, price, or impelling influence which induces a contracting party to enter into a contract. The reason or material cause of a contract. An act or forbearance, or the promise thereof, which is offered by one party to an agreement, and accepted by the other as an inducement to that other's act or promise.

Constructive Service: (Of Process) Any form of service other than actual personal service; notification of an action or of some proceeding therein, given to a person affected by sending it to him in the mails or causing it to be published in a newspaper.

Contempt: A willful disregard or disobedience of a public authority.

Contract: An oral, written, or implied agreement between two or more persons; a formal covenent of undertaking; an enforceable pact.

Contributory Negligence: The act or omission amounting to want of ordinary care on the part of complaining party, which, concurring with the defendant's negligence, is the proximate cause of injury.

Controversy: A litigated question; adversary proceeding in a court of law; a civil action or suit, either at law or in equity; a justiciable dispute. It differs from "case," which includes all suits, criminal as well as civil; whereas "controversy" is a civil and not a criminal proceeding.

Controvert: To dispute; to deny; to oppose or contest; to take issue on.

Corporation: A number of persons united or regarded as united in one body; an artificial person, created by law, or under authority of law, from a group or succession of natural persons, and having a continuous existence irrespective of that of its members, and powers and liabilities distinct from those of its members.

Counsel: 1. An advocate, counsellor, or pleader. One who assists his client with advice, and pleads for him in open court. One who has been admitted as an attorney and counsellor at law. 2. Advice given by one person to another in regard to a proposed line of conduct, claim, or contention.

Counterclaim: A claim presented by a defendant in opposition to or deduction from the claim of the plaintiff. A species of set-off or recoupment introduced by the codes of civil procedure in many of the states, of a broad and liberal character.

Court: An organ of the government, belonging to the judicial department, whose function is the application of the laws to controversies brought before it and the public administration of justice.

Court Reporter: In trial courts, a person who transcribes the testimony and proceedings in a trial or proceedings before the court.

Credibility: Worthiness of belief; that quality in a witness which renders his evidence worthy of belief. After the competence of a witness is allowed, the consideration of his credibility arises, and not before.

Criminal: 1. One who has committed a criminal offense; one who has been legally convicted of a crime; one adjudged guilty of crime. 2. That which pertains to or is connected with the law of crimes, or the administration of penal justice, or which relates to or has the character of crime.

Cross-Claim: A "cross-claim" is one brought by a defendant against a plaintiff in the same action or against a plaintiff in the same action or against a co-defendant or both concerning matters in question in the original complaint, and its purposes are to discover facts in aid of defense, to bring in new matter in aid of defense, to obtain some affirmative relief concerning matters in issue, to obtain full relief for all parties and a complete determination of all controversies arising out of matters alleged in the original complaint, and to have affirmative relief against either plaintiff or co-defendant in the nature of an original complaint.

Cross-Complaint: In some state courts, an action brought by a defendant against plaintiff or co-defendant. Generally, in most courts, is is called a cross-claim.

Cross-examination: The examination of a witness upon a trial or hearing, or upon taking a deposition, by the party opposed to the one who produced him, upon his evidence given in chief, to test its truth, to further develop it, or for other purposes.

Default: Omission; neglect or failure of any party to take steps required of him in progress of cause. When a defendant in an action at law omits to plead within the time allowed him for that purpose, or fails to appear on the trial, he is said to make default, and the judgment entered in the former case is technically called a "judgment by default."

Defendant: The person defending or denying; the party against whom relief or recovery is sought in an action or suit.

Defense: That which is offered and alleged by a party proceeded against in an action or suit, as a reason in law or fact why the plaintiff should not recover or establish what he seeks; what is put forward to diminish plaintiff's cause of action or defeat recovery.

Demurrer: A formal mode of disputing the sufficiency in law of the pleading of the other side. In effect it is an allegation that, even if the facts as stated in the pleading to which objection is taken be true, yet their legal consequences are not such as to put the demurring party to the necessity of answering them or proceeding further with the cause.

Deposition: The testimony of a witness taken upon interrogatories, not in open court, but in pursuance of a commission to take testimony issued by a court, or under a general law on the subject, and reduced to writing and duly authenticated, and intended to be used upon the trial of an action in court.

Dilatory Defense: A defense that does not go to the merits of the case, but rather attempts to delay the action until the obstacle is removed.

Directed Verdict: A verdict rendered by the jury, at the direction of the court, where the evidence is insufficient, where the overwhelming weight of the evidence is for one party, or where the law as applied to the facts demands such a verdict.

Discharge in Bankruptcy: The discharge of the bankrupt is the step which regularly follows the adjudication of bankruptcy and the administration of his estate. By it he is released from the obligations of all his debts which were or might be proved in the proceedings, so that they are no longer a charge upon him, and so that he may thereafter engage in business and acquire property without his being liable for the satisfaction of such former debts.

Discovery: The disclosure by a litigant of facts, titles, documents, or other things which are in his exclusive knowledge or possession, and which are necessary to the party seeking the discovery as a part of a cause or action pending or to be brought in another court, or as evidence of his rights or title in such proceeding.

Diversity Jurisdiction: A term used with reference to the jurisdiction of the federal courts, which, under the United States Constitution, extends to cases between citizens of different states, designating the condition existing when the party on the other side is a citizen of another state. When this is the basis of jurisdiction all the persons on one side of the controversy must be citizens of different states from all the persons on the other side.

Duress: Unlawful constraint exercised upon a person whereby he is forced to so some act that he otherwise would not have done. It consists in an illegal imprisonment, or legal imprisonment used for an illegal purpose, or threats of bodily or other harm, or other means amounting to or tending to coerce the will of another, and actually inducing him to do an act contrary to his free will. It is never "duress" to threaten to do that which a party has a legal right to do.

Equity: The quality of being fair or impartial; fairness; a system of jurisprudence that includes a body of legal rules and doctrines determining what is equitable and fair, which supplements and remedies the defects of common and statutory law; any system of jurisprudence incorporating such a body of supplementary and remedial rules and doctrines; an equitable right or claim.

Escobedo Rule: When an investigation begins to focus on a particular suspect, and the police take the suspect into custody to elicit incriminating testimony, the suspect must be warned of his right to remain silent and to consult with an attorney. If these provisions are not met, the Escobedo Rule maintains that no statement made by the suspect while being interrogated may be used against him in a criminal action. Escobedo v. Illinois, 378 U.S. 478 (1964).

Estoppel: An estoppel arises when one is precluded and forbidden by law to speak against his own act or deed. An inconsistent position, attitude or course of conduct may not be adopted to the loss or injury of another. Under the law of estoppel where one of two innocent persons must suffer, he whose act occasioned loss must bear it.

Evidence: Any species of proof, or probative matter, legally presented at the trial of an issue, by the act of the parties and through the medium of witnesses, records, documents, concrete objects, etc., for the purpose of inducing belief in the minds of the court or jury as to their contentions.

Ex Parte: On one side only; by or for one party; done for, in behalf of, or on the application of, one party only.

Failure of Consideration: As applied to notes, contracts, conveyances, etc., this term does not mean a want of consideration, but implies that a consideration, originally existing and good, has since become worthless or has ceased to exist or been extinguished, partially or entirely.

Faretta Case: U. S. Supreme Court decision which held that a state cannot "constitutionally hale a person into its criminal courts and there force a lawyer upon him, even when he insists that he wants to conduct his own defense. Faretta v. California, 422 U.S. 806 (1975).

Forum non Conveniens: The doctrine is patterned upon the right of the court in the exercise of its equitable powers to refuse the imposition upon its jurisdiction of the trial of cases even though the venue is properly laid if it appears that for the convenience of litigants and witnesses and in the interest of justice the action should be instituted in another forum where the action might have been brought. The doctrine presupposes at least two forums in which the defendant is amenable to process and furnishes criteria for choice between such forums.

Fourteenth Amendment: (U. S. Constitution) It became a part of the organic law July 28, 1868, and its importance entitles it to special mention. It creates or at least recognizes for the first time a citizenship of the United States, as distinct from that of the states; forbids the making or enforcement by any state of any law abridging the privileges and immunities of citizens of the United States; and secures all "persons" against any state action which is either deprivation of life, liberty, or property without due process of law or denial of equal protection of the laws.

Fraud: An intentional perversion of truth for the purpose of inducing another, in reliance upon it, to part with some valuable thing belonging to him or to surrender a legal right; a false representation of a matter of face, whether by words or by conduct, by false or misleading representations, or by concealment of that which should have been disclosed, which deceives, and is intended to deceive another so that he shall act upon it to his legal detriment.

Frivolous: An answer is "frivolous" where it appears from bare inspection to be lacking in legal sufficiency, and, where in any view of the facts pleaded, it does not present a defense. Any pleading is called "frivolous" when it is clearly insufficient on its face, and does not controvert the material points of the opposite pleading, and is presumably interposed for mere purposes of delay or to embarrass the opponent.

Garnishment: See Writ of,

Golden Rule Argument: Argument to a jury to "put yourselves in the place of" one of the parties. It is improper because the jury is by law required to be objective and fair to all parties.

Hearing: Proceeding of relative formality, generally public, with definite issues of fact or of law to be tried, in which parties proceeded against have a right to be heard, and is much the same as a trial and may terminate in final order. The word is synonymous with trial, and includes the reception of evidence and arguments thereon.

Hearsay: Evidence not proceeding from the personal knowledge of the witness, but from the mere repetition of what he has heard others say. That which does not derive its value solely from the credit of the witness, but rests mainly on the veracity and competency of other persons. The very nature of the evidence shows its weakness, and it is admitted only in specified cases from necessity. It is second-hand evidence, as distinguished from original evidence; it is the repetition at second-hand of what would be original evidence if given by the person who originally made the statement. Literally, it is what the witness says he heard another person say.

Illegality: That which is contrary to the principles of law, as distinguished from mere rules of procedure. It denotes a complete defect in the proceedings.

Immaterial: Not material, essential, or necessary; not important or pertinent; not decisive; of no substantial consequence; without weight; of no significance.

Impertinent: That which does not belong to a pleading, interrogatory or other proceeding; out of place; superfluous; irrelevant. A term applied to matter not necessary to constitute the cause of action or ground of defense. It constitutes surplusage.

Inference: A truth or proposition drawn from another which is supposed or admitted to be true. A process of reasoning by which a fact or proposition sought to be established is deducted as a logical consequence from the other facts, or a state of facts, already proved or admitted.

Injunction: A prohibitive writ issued by a court directed to a party in the action, or to a party made a party for that purpose, forbidding the latter to do some act, or to permit his servants or agents to do some act, which he is threatening or attempting to commit, or restraining him in a continuance thereof, such act being unjust and inequitable, injurious to the plaintiff, and not such as can be adequately redressed by an action at law. A judicial process operating in personam, and requiring a person to whom it is directed to do or refrain from doing a particular thing.

In rem: A technical term used to designate proceedings or actions against the thing, in contradistinction to personal actions, which are said to be in personam.

Institute: To inaugurate or commence; as to institute an action.

Interrogatory: A set or series of written questions drawn up and propounded by one party and served on an adversary, who must serve written answers thereto under oath.

Jurisdiction: The word is a term of large and comprehensive import, and embraces every kind of judicial action. It is the authority by which courts and judicial officers take cognizance of and decide cases; the legal right by which judges exercise their authority. It exists when court has cognizance of class of cases involved, proper parties are present, and point to be decided is within issues.

Jury: A certain number of men or women, selected according to law, and sworn to inquire of certain matters of face, and declare the truth upon evidence to be laid before them. This definition embraces the various subdivisions of juries.

Laches: Laches is, or is based on, delay attended by or inducing change of condition or relation. Estoppel by laches means a failure to do something which should be done or to claim or enforce a right at a proper time. A neglect to do something which one should do, or to seek to enforce a right at a proper time.

Lack of Jurisdiction: The phrase may mean lack of power to act in a particular manner or to give certain kinds of relief. It may consist in the court's total want of power to act at all, or lack of power to act in particular cases because conditions essential to exercise of jurisdiction have not been complied with.

Liable: Answerable for consequences; under obligation legally to make good a loss; responsible; apt or likely to incur something undesirable; susceptible; subject or exposed to.

Lien: A claim or charge on property for payment of some debt, obligation or duty.

Litigation: Contest in a court of justice for the purpose of enforcing a right. A judicial contest, a judicial controversy, a suit at law; a civil action.

Long Arm Statute: A statute allowing a court to obtain jurisdiction over a defendant located outside the normal jurisdiction of the court.

Miranda Rule: When a person is taken into custody, and prior to any interrogation, he must be warned that he has the right to remain silent, that any statement he makes may be used against him, that he has the right to speak to an attorney, and that if he cannot afford an attorney one will be appointed for him if he so desires. Unless these warnings are given or the rights are waived, the Miranda Rule maintains that no evidence obtained from an interrogation is allowed in court. Miranda v. Arizona, 384 U.S. 346 (1966).

Misrepresentation: Any manifestation by words or other conduct by one person to another that, under the circumstances, amounts to an assertion not in accordance with the facts. An untrue statement of fact. An incorrect or false representation. That which, if accepted, leads the mind to an apprehension of a condition other and different from that which exists. False and fraudulent misrepresentation is a representation contrary to the fact, made by a person with a knowledge of its falsehood, and being the cause of the other party's entering into the contract. Negligent misrepresentation is a false representation made by a person who has no reasonable grounds for believing it to be true, though he does not know that it is untrue, or even believes it to be true.

Mistrial: An erroneous, invalid, or nugatory trial; a trial of an action which cannot stand in law because of want of jurisdiction, or a wrong drawing of jurors, or disregard of some other fundamental requisite.

Motion: An application for an order to a court or judge; a motion addressed to the discretion of the court.

Negligence: The omission to do something which a reasonable man, guided by those ordinary considerations which ordinarily regulate human affairs, would do, or the doing of something which a reasonable and prudent man would not do.

Notary Public: A public officer whose function it is to administer oaths; to attest and certify, by his hand and official seal, certain classes of documents, in order to give them credit and authenticity; to take acknowledgment of deeds and other conveyances, and certify the same; and to perform certain other official acts.

Partnership: A voluntary contract between two or more competent persons to place their money, effects, labor, and skill, or some or all of them, in lawful commerce or business, with the understanding that there shall be a proportional sharing of the profits and losses between them. An association of two or more persons to carry on as co-owners of a business for profit.

Payment: The fulfillment of a promise, or the performance of an agreement; a discharge of an obligation or debt, and part payment, if accepted, is a discharge pro tanto (as far as it goes).

Perjury: The willful assertion as to a matter of fact, opinion, belief, or knowledge, made by a witness in a judicial proceeding as part of his evidence, either upon oath or in any form allowed by law to be substituted for an oath, whether such evidence is given in open court, or in an affidavit, or otherwise, such assertion being material to the issue or point of inquiry and known to such witness to be false.

Permissive Counterclaim: An action by a defendant against a plaintiff arising out of a "transaction or occurrence" not the same as the subject of a claim of plaintiff against the defendant.

Petition: An application made to a court ex parte, or where there are no parties in opposition, praying for the exercise of the judicial powers of the court in relation to some matter which is not the subject for a suit or action, or for authority to do some act which requires the sanction of the court; as for the appointment of a guardian, for leave to sell trust property, etc.

Plaintiff: A person who brings an action; the party who complains or sues in a personal action and is so named on the record.

Pleading: The formal allegations by the parties of their respective claims and defenses, for the judgment of the court.

Preemptory Challenge: A challenge to a prospective juror, in jury selection, disqualifying him from being empaneled for no stated reason. The number of preemptory challenges varies and is established by statute.

Prejudice: A forejudgment; bias, preconceived opinion. A leaning towards one side of a cause for some reason other than a conviction of its justice.

Preponderance of Evidence: Greater weight of evidence, or evidence which is more credible and convincing to the mind. That which best accords with reason and probability. The word "preponderance" means something more than "weight;" it denotes a superiority of weight, or outweighing. The words are not synonymous, but substantially different. There is generally "weight" of evidence on each side in case of contested facts. But juries cannot properly act upon the weight of evidence, in favor of one having the onus, unless it overbears, in some degree, the weight upon the other side.

Prima Facie Case: Such as will suffice until contradicted and overcome by other evidence. A case which has proceeded upon sufficient proof to that stage where it will support finding if evidence to contrary is disregarded.

Probate: The act or process of proving a will. The proof before an ordinary, surrogate, register, or other duly authorized person that a document produced before him for official recognition and registration, and alleged to be the last will and testament of a certain deceased person, is such in reality. A judicial act or determination of a court having competent jurisdiction establishing the validity of a will.

Procedural Law: That which prescribes method of enforcing rights or obtaining redress for their invasion;

machinery for carrying on a suit.

Pro Se: For himself; in his own behalf; in person.

Rebuttal: The introduction of rebuttal evidence; the showing that statement of witnesses as to what occurred is not true; the stage of a trial at which such evidence may be introduced; also the rebutting evidence itself.

Redundancy: This is the fault of introducing superfluous matter into a legal instrument; particularly the insertion in a pleading of matters foreign, extraneous, and irrelevant to that which it is intended to answer.

Release: The relinquishment, concession, or giving up of a right, claim, or privilege, by the person in whom it exists or to whom it accrues, to the person against whom it might have been demanded or enforced.

Reply: In its general sense, that which a plaintiff, or other party who has instituted a proceeding says in answer to the defendant's counterclaim or answer.

Res: A thing; an object. As a term of the law, this word has a very wide and extensive signification, including not only things which are objects of property, but also such as are not capable of individual ownership.

Res Ipsa Loquitor: The thing speaks for itself. Rebuttable presumption that defendant was negligent, which arises upon proof that instrumentality causing injury was in defendant's exclusive control, and that the accident was one which ordinarily does not happen in absence of negligence.

Res Judicata: A matter adjudged; a thing judicially acted upon or decided; a thing or matter settled by judgment.

Rule 12 Motions: The pleadings and motions authorized by Federal Rule 12 and those state rules patterned after it. See discussion in Chapter III.

Scintilla: Latin word meaning spark; a remaining particle; the least particle.

Scintilla of Evidence: A spark of evidence. A metaphorical expression to describe a very insignificant or trifling item or particle of evidence; used in the statement of the common law rule that if there is any evidence at all in a case, even a mere scintilla, tending to support a material issue, the case cannot be taken from the jury, but must be left to their decision.

Secondary Evidence: That which is inferior to primary. Thus, a copy of an instrument, or oral evidence of its contents, is secondary evidence of the instrument and contents. It is that species of evidence which becomes admissible, as being the next best, when the primary or best evidence of the fact in question is lost or inaccessible; as when a witness details orally the contents of an instrument which is lost or destroyed.

Second-hand Evidence: Evidence which has passed through one or more media before reaching the witness; hearsay evidence.

Service of Process: The service of writs, summonses, rules, etc., signifies the delivering to or leaving them with the party to whom or with whom they ought to be delivered or left; and, when they are so delivered, they are then said to have been served. Usually a copy only is served and the original is shown.

Shyster: A trickish knave; one who carries on any business, especially a legal business, in a dishonest way. An unscrupulous practitioner who disgraces his profession by doing mean work, and resorts to sharp practice to do it.

Slander: The speaking of base and defamatory words tending to prejudice another in his reputation, office, trade, business, or means of livelihood.

Special Appearance: A submission to the jurisdiction of a court for some special purpose only, such as a contest of jurisdiction or sufficiency of evidence.

Statute: An act of the legislature declaring, commanding, or prohibiting something; a particular law enacted and established by the will of the legislature; the written will of the legislature, solemnly expressed according to the forms necessary to constitute it the law of the state.

Statute of Frauds: This is the common designation of a very celebrated English statute (29 Car. II. C. 3,) passed in 1677, and which has been adopted in a more or less modified form, in all states in this country. Its chief characteristic is the provision that no suit or action shall be maintained on certain classes of contracts or engagements unless there shall be a note or memorandum thereof in writing signed by the party to be charged or by his authorized agent. Its object was to close the door to the numerous frauds and perjuries.

Statute of Limitations: A statute imposing limits on the period during which certain rights, as the collection of debts, may be legally enforced.

Strict Liability: Liability without fault. A case is one of "strict liability" when neither care nor negligence, neither good nor bad faith, neither knowledge nor ignorance will save defendant.

Subpoena: A process to cause a witness to appear and give testimony, commanding him to lay aside all pretenses and excuses, and appear before a court or magistrate therein named at a time therein mentioned to testify for the party named under penalty therein mentioned.

Substantive Law: That part of law which creates, defines, and regulates rights, as opposed to "adjective or remedial law," which prescribes method of enforcing the rights or obtaining redress for their invasion.

Substituted Service: Service of process upon a defendant in any manner, authorized by statute, other than personal service within the jurisdiction; as by publication, by mailing a copy to his last known address, or by personal service in another state.

Summation: On the trial of an action by a jury, a recapitulation of the evidence adduced, in order to draw the attention of the jury to the salient points. The counsel for each party has the right of summing up his evidence, if he has adduced any, and the judge sometimes sums up the whole in his charge to the jury.

Summary Judgment: A judgment rendered on a motion by a party to a lawsuit, where pleadings, depositions, interrogatories, admissions, and other evidence show that there is no issue as to any material fact, and that the movant is entitled to a judgment as a matter of law. See Rule 56.

Summons: A writ, directed to the sheriff or other proper officer, requiring him to notify the person named that an action has been commenced against him in the court whence the writ issued, and that he is required to appear, on a day named, and answer the complaint in such action.

Tort: A private or civil wrong or injury. A wrong independent of contract. A violation of a duty imposed by general law or otherwise upon all persons occupying the relation to each other which is involved in a given transaction.

Trial: A judicial examination, in accordance with the law of the land, of a cause, either civil or criminal, of the issues between the parties, whether of law or fact, before a court that has jurisdiction over it.

Usury: An illegal contract for a loan or forbearance of money, goods, or things in action, by which illegal interest is reserved, or agreed to be reserved or taken. An unconscionable and exorbitant rate or amount of interest.

Venue: A neighborhood; the place, or county in which an injury is declared to have been done, or fact declared to have happened. A venue which must be laid in a particular county.

Verdict: From the Latin "ceredictum," a true declaration. The formal finding made by a jury, impaneled and sworn for the trial of a cause, and reported to the court (and accepted by it), upon the matters or questions duly submitted to them upon the trial.

Void: Having no legal or binding force; null. Empty or not containing matter; vacant; unoccupied; devoid; destitute.

Waiver: The intentional or voluntary relinquishment of a known right, or such conduct as warrants an inference of the relinquishment of such right. The renunciation, repudiation, abandonment, or surrender of some claim, right, privilege, or of the opportunity to take advantage of some defect, irregularity, or wrong.

Witness: One who, being present, personally sees or perceives a thing; a beholder, spectator, or eyewitness. One who testifies to what he has seen, heard, or otherwise observed.

Writ of Attachment: A writ employed to enforce obedience to an order or judgment of the court. It may take the form of commanding the sheriff to attach the disobedient party and to have him before the court to answer his contempt.

Writ of Error Coram Nobis: A common law writ, the purpose of which is to correct a judgment in the same court in which it was rendered, on the ground of error of fact.

Writ of Execution: A writ to put in force the judgment or decree of a court.

Writ of Garnishment: A warning to a person in whose hands the effects of another are attached, not to pay the money or deliver the property of the defendant in his hands to him, but to appear and answer the plaintiff's suit. A statutory proceeding whereby a person's property, money, or credits in possession or under control of, or owing by, another are applied to payment of former's debt to third person by proper statutory process against debtor and garnishee.

APPENDIX

BIBLIOGRAPHY OF LAW BOOKS

American Jurisprudence, Second (Am Jur 2d)
Am Jur, Legal Forms
Am Jur, Pleading and Practice Forms
Am Jur, Proof of Facts
Am Jur, Trials
American Law Reports (ALR)
ALR 2d
ALR 3d
ALR FED
Bender, Federal Practice Manual
Bender, Federal Practice Forms
Bender, Forms of Discovery
Black's Law Dictionary, Fourth Edition
Corpus Juris Secondum (C.J.S.)
California Discovery Practice
California Pretrial and Settlement Procedures
California Procedures, Second
Federal Civil Practice, Harold A. Kooman
Federal Jury Practice and Instructions, Second, 1970
Federal Practice Digest
Federal Practice & Procedure, Barron & Holtzoff
Florida Civil Practice Before Trial, Third CLE (1975)
Interrogatories: Basic Facts, Douglas Danner 1970
Jury Instructions (Your State)
Law of Evidence, Charles T. McCormick
Law of Federal Courts, Second, 1970, Charles Allen Wright
Martindale-Hubbell Law Digest, Volume VI
New York Civil Practice, Weinstein & Korn
United States Code Annotated
United States Code Service
Words and Phrases

West Report System:

Atlantic Reports; and A 2d:	CT,DE, DC, ME, MD, NH, NJ, PA, RI, VT
Northeastern Reports; and N.E. 2d:	IL, IN, MA, NY, OH
Northwestern Reports; and N.W. 2d:	IA, MI, MN, NE, SD, WI
Pacific Reports; and P 2d:	AK, AZ, CA, CO, HI, ID, KS, MT, NV, NM, OK, OR, UT, WA, WY
Southeastern Reports; and S.E. 2d:	GA, SC, NC, VA, WV
Southwestern Reports; and S.W. 2d:	AR, MO, KY, TN, TX
Southern Reports; and So 2d:	AL, LA, FL, MS

Supreme Court Reports; Federal Reports, F 2d, Federal Supplement

INDEX